Passport's Illustrated Travel Guide to

BALI & JAVA

D1519409

FROM
THOMAS COOK

PASSPORT BOOKS
a division of *NTC Publishing Group*
Lincolnwood, Illinois USA

Published by Passport Books,
a division of NTC Publishing Group,
4255 W. Touhy Avenue,
Lincolnwood (Chicago), Illinois
60646–1975 U.S.A.

Written by Ben Davies

Original photography by Ben Davies

Edited, designed and produced by AA Publishing.
© The Automobile Association 1995.
Maps © The Automobile Association 1995.

Library of Congress Catalog Card Number: 94-68181

ISBN 0-8442-9081-5

The contents of this publication are believed correct at the time of
printing. Nevertheless, the publishers cannot accept responsibility for
any errors or omissions, or for changes in the details given in this guide
or for the consequences of any reliance on the information provided by
the same. Assessments of attractions, hotels, restaurants and so forth are
based upon the author's own experience and therefore descriptions given
in this guide necessarily contain an element of subjective opinion which
may not reflect the publisher's opinion or dictate a reader's own
experiences on another occasion.
We have tried to ensure accuracy in this guide, but things do
change and we would be grateful if readers would advise us of any
inaccuracies they may encounter.

Published by Passport Books in conjunction with AA Publishing and the
Thomas Cook Group Ltd.

Color separation: BTB Colour Reproduction, Whitchurch, Hampshire,
England.

Printed by: Edicoes ASA, Oporto, Portugal.

Contents

About this Book

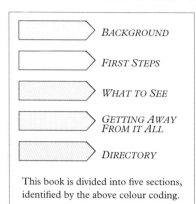

BACKGROUND

FIRST STEPS

WHAT TO SEE

GETTING AWAY
FROM IT ALL

DIRECTORY

This book is divided into five sections,
identified by the above colour coding.

Background gives an introduction to
Bali, Java and Lombok – their history,
geography, politics, culture.

First Steps offers practical advice on
arriving and getting around.
What to See is an alphabetical listing of
places to visit, interspersed with walks
and tours.
Getting Away From it All highlights
places off the beaten track where it is
possible to relax and enjoy peace and
quiet.
Finally, the **Directory** provides practical
information – from shopping and
entertainment to children and sport,
including a section on business matters.
Special highly illustrated *features* on
specific aspects of Bali, Java and
Lombok appear throughout the book.

Magnificent stone carvings are scattered
throughout Bali

BACKGROUND

'Hurled onto the shores of Bali, we had, though we knew it not,
reached one of the most fantastic places of the earth.'

VIOLET CLIFTON
Islands of Indonesia (1927)

Introduction

Scattered among the tropical waters of the Indian Ocean, with their palm-fringed beaches and fiery volcanoes, the 13,677 islands that make up the Indonesian archipelago offer visitors some of the most beautiful and exotic destinations in the world – as well as an abundance of culture.

Indonesia has magnificent temples and teeming cities along with thousands of different species of wildlife ranging from orchids to tigers to strawberries.

Ethnically, too, the country is made up of a hugely diverse population, speaking some 300 different languages and drawn from as far afield as India and the Pacific. And whilst some 87 per cent of the people are Muslim, there is room for Hindus, animists and Christians too, amongst others.

Each island, from the legendary Bali, home of the gods, to Sumatra and Irian Jaya with their exotic jungles, is a world of its own offering something a little special. On Lombok, you can climb Mount Rinjani, one of the most spectacular volcanoes in the country, and on Java visit the 1,000-year-old temple of Borobudur. Sun-lovers on Bali can take

The majority of the Indonesian people still earn their living by working the fields

BALI, JAVA & LOMBOK

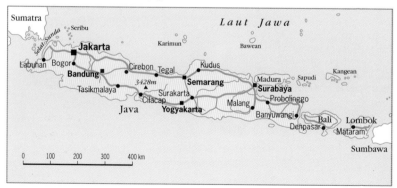

SOUTHEAST ASIA

their pick from a star-studded list of glistening white beaches, as well as luxury hotels and discothèques, and in Jakarta visitors can revel in some of the most chaotic scenes in the world.

Nor is it only the diverse scenery that will delight. In Indonesia you can feast on mouthwatering foods ranging from fresh lobster to *satay* – grilled meat served with peanut sauce. The adventurous can even try Indonesia's *pièce de résistance*, barbecued mutton brain.

Shoppers, too, can take their pick of hand-woven baskets, leather puppets and colourful batiks. And then there are the people: shy, playful, in some areas merely resigned to tourists, in others welcoming them with a ready smile.

THOMAS COOK'S
Bali, Java and Lombok

The first record of a Cook's excursion to Java was in 1909, when it formed part of a three-month personally conducted tour. At that time the island was known as 'the Garden of the East' and visitors were conveyed there from Singapore by luxurious steamer – a journey taking 40 hours.

History

c.700,000–200,000BP
Fossils discovered in 1891 of the so-called 'Java man' near the village of Trinil prove that Indonesia played host to early *Homo erectus*.

3000–500BC
Successive waves of migrants arrive from South China and Tonkin.

1st century AD
Indonesia comes under the influence of Indian trade and culture, paving the way for a succession of Indianised kingdoms.

8th–10th century
One of the greatest and most powerful kingdoms is established in Central Java by the Buddhist Sailendra dynasty.

778–856
Construction of the magnificent Borobudur temple by the Sailendras.

8th–11th century
The Hindu Sanjaya dynasty holds sway over parts of Central and East Java, building the famous Prambanan temples.

1222–1292
King Angrok establishes the Singasari dynasty which holds power in East Java, and the Malay Peninsula.

1292
Marco Polo becomes the first European to set foot in Indonesia when he visits Sumatra.

1292–1478
Rise of the powerful Hindu empire of Majapahit, which dominates much of Indonesia and parts of neighbouring Malaysia.

1343
Javanese colony established on Bali.

1400
Islam first introduced to Indonesia. By the end of the 16th century it replaces Hinduism and Buddhism as the dominant religion.

1522
The Portuguese establish trading posts in the Spice Islands and at Sunda Kelapa to control the lucrative spice trade.

1528
Foundation of Jakarta, known as Jayakarta.

1572–1757
The last great Javanese kingdom of Mataram holds sway around Yogyakarta and Surakarta.

1619
The Dutch East India Company takes Jayakarta by force and renames the town Batavia. Gradually they establish trading posts throughout Java.

1628–29
Sultan Agung, the most famous ruler of Mataram, attacks Batavia but fails to dislodge the Dutch.

1811
Following the Napoleonic Wars, the British take control of Batavia under Lieutenant-Governor Sir Thomas Stamford Raffles.

1816
Raffles and the British are ousted by the Dutch.

1825
Prince Diponegoro, son of the Sultan of Yogyakarta, leads a revolt against the Dutch. After five years he is defeated and exiled to Sulawesi.

1894
Dutch military victory on Lombok.

1906
Dutch troops land at Sanur Beach on Bali. The princely families of Badung and Tabanan refuse to surrender and

more than 4,000 of them commit *puputan*, or mass suicide.

1911
The Dutch establish control over all the Indonesian islands except East Timor and North Borneo.

1914–1918
World War I. Growing nationalist sentiment takes hold in Indonesia.

1927
Foundation of the Patai Nasional Indonesia, a political party aimed at securing independence.

1942–45
The Japanese occupy Indonesia. Initially they are welcomed as liberators. Later the people turn against them.

1945
Indonesia proclaims its independence, but the Dutch refuse to accept the declaration.

1945
Yogyakarta declared capital of the founding republic.

1948
The Dutch capture Yogyakarta, prompting a guerrilla campaign in rural areas.

1949
The Dutch are ordered to withdraw from Indonesia by the United Nations and a new republic is officially proclaimed.

Soekarno becomes first president of the Republic of Indonesia.

1950–65
Economic and social problems are compounded by domestic unrest and growing support for the communists.

1965
Six army generals are murdered in an attempted *coup d'état* blamed on the communist party. General Suharto, chief of the Army Strategic Reserve Command, takes control.

1967–8
Soekarno is placed under house arrest and Suharto is inaugurated as president. Thousands of alleged communists are killed throughout the country, especially on Bali.

1970–1980
Growing economic prosperity brought about by rising oil prices leads to corruption on a scale almost unparalleled. Continuing unrest in outlying areas.

1989–1992
Suharto liberalises foreign investment regulations and presides over a period of rapid growth. Western observers herald the beginnings of a new economic giant.

1991
Massacre in East Timor.

1992
Golkar, which is the state party, wins its sixth consecutive victory, gaining 68 per cent of the vote.

1993
Suharto is reappointed president for his sixth, and probably his last, five-year term.

Medan Merdeka, Jakarta

Geography

*I*ndonesia offers a vast choice of landscape, spread over one of the largest and most diverse areas in the world. In total the country covers almost 10 million sq km, stretching more than 5,500km from its northwestern tip in Sumatra to the coast of Irian Jaya in the south. This equates to one eighth of the circumference of the globe, or 46 degrees of latitude. Furthermore, Indonesia is one of the only countries in the world which has more sea than land; the total area occupied by Indonesia's surrounding seas and oceans is greater than the total area occupied by its 13,677 islands.

Covering the land mass is a wide range of terrain, from steep mountains and rain forests to steaming lowlands and equatorial vegetation. On top of that, Indonesia boasts some 300 volcanoes, 100 of which still rumble and erupt with relentless predictability.

You will find plenty of geological wonders, too, from lakes filled with sulphurous waters to vast calderas, as well as some of the most fertile soil on earth – from the sky, the terraced rice fields on Bali and Java resemble a giant patchwork quilt that stretches as far as the eye can see. Don't expect to see too much wildlife though. Most of the tigers

disappeared many years ago, making way for the endless march of Indonesia's population.

Economy

Potentially one of the richest countries in the world, Indonesia has almost every resource in abundance, from palm oil to rubber, timber, oil, gas, tea, coffee and spices. Its rich soil and abundant workforce produces rice enough to feed the country's 185 million population. These days, with its vast pool of cheap labour, the country also churns out textiles, computer chips and car components.

The one thing that Indonesia doesn't have, however, is evenly distributed wealth. Whilst the rich own huge tracts of land, many of the poor live in shacks and cardboard houses. Indonesia has more than its share of millionaires, but the average income per capita is little more than US$500 a year, with 17 per cent of the population on the poverty line.

But even that is changing. The arrival of foreign investors has rapidly turned Indonesia's economy into one of the fastest moving in the world, growing two or three times faster every year than

Farming the slopes high up in the hills of the Sarangan

Bali hosts some of the most intricately constructed rice fields in the world

countries in Europe. And while rice and agriculture are likely to continue to dominate the lives of many rural inhabitants, growing numbers of people are being lured into the towns and cities in search of work, prosperity and a taste of the 20th century.

Climate
In Indonesia's equatorial climate you are unlikely to suffer from excessive cold, unless you spend the night on top of a mountain, but you may find yourself inundated with tropical rains. This is especially true in the months between November and April when much of the country's 2,000mm annual rainfall occurs. The dry season tends to last from May to October, generally with clear blue skies and only occasional showers. Not surprisingly, this is when most tourists visit the country. Temperatures remain remarkably constant throughout the year, averaging about 26°C. Only in the months before the monsoon is humidity high.

Population
More than 185 million people crowd the teeming islands of Indonesia, making this vast archipelago the fourth most populated country in the world. Nor is the rate of increase slowing down. Every year the population increases by 2.2 per cent and lack of jobs means that millions of school leavers are unable to find work. On Java especially the population has reached frightening proportions and now ranks as one of the densest in the world, with over 1,500 people per sq km. Bali's total population is estimated at around 2.7 million, equating to a mere 500 people per sq km, while the total population of Lombok is put at 2.5 million.

PEOPLES OF BALI, JAVA AND LOMBOK

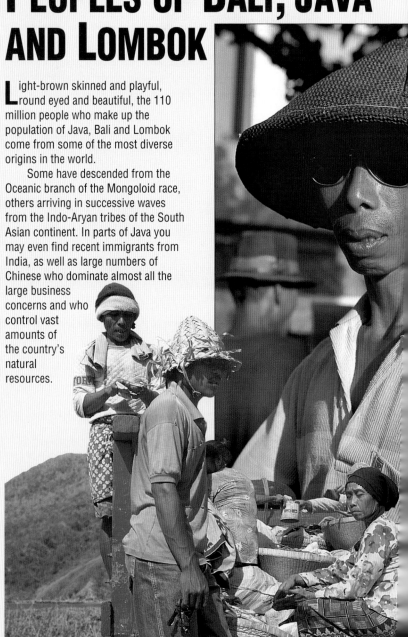

Light-brown skinned and playful, round eyed and beautiful, the 110 million people who make up the population of Java, Bali and Lombok come from some of the most diverse origins in the world.

Some have descended from the Oceanic branch of the Mongoloid race, others arriving in successive waves from the Indo-Aryan tribes of the South Asian continent. In parts of Java you may even find recent immigrants from India, as well as large numbers of Chinese who dominate almost all the large business concerns and who control vast amounts of the country's natural resources.

The Indonesian people not only pride themselves on their different origins, but in many cases have their own distinctive culture, their own language and history. The Badui of West Java have remained aloof from the modern world, recognising no government and forbidding strangers to spend the night in their villages. Others, like the Tenggerese, have intermingled and embraced the Indonesian principles of *Pancasila*, or national unity and social justice. But whatever their origins, these people all share one thing in common: their home is one of the most diverse and fertile countries in the world.

Culture

*F*rom classical dancers to glittering palaces and temples and colourful batiks, Indonesia offers a wealth and breadth of culture almost beyond compare. On Bali alone you will find an estimated 20,000 temples serving the island's 2.7 million population, while on Java, nearly every town or village has at least one mosque. On top of that are literally thousands of ceremonies, festivals and cremations as well as a complex set of rituals that influence almost every aspect of life throughout the teeming archipelago.

Religions

Islam is the predominant religion in Indonesia. In total, some 87 per cent of the population are Muslim, making this the world's largest Islamic nation. But Indonesia also spawns a variety of other religions from Buddhism to Hinduism and even Christianity.

The largest concentration of Muslims is to be found in Java and on the island of Lombok, home to the Sasak people. Crossing the narrow straits to Bali, you move to a world of good and evil spirits, of rain gods, rice gods and the endless circle of death and rebirth. Hinduism was brought to this island sometime during the 5th century by pilgrims from India. Today the religion has been influenced by Buddhism and animism and absorbed into everyday life.

Daily Life

Whatever the religion, ritual plays a crucial role. As well as the greater duties of a pilgrimage to Mecca, all good Muslims must pray five times a day, give alms to the poor, and fast during daylight hours in the holy month of Ramadan. The Balinese Hindus, who worship Tintaya, Brahma the creator, Shiva the destroyer and Vishnu the preserver, must also make daily offerings to, and tend the shrines of, their ancestors, Dewi Sri goddess of rice, Dewi Ratih, goddess of the moon and even Dewi Melanting, goddess of shopkeeping. Together with a host of other spirits, these provide not only the key to their spiritual life but the greater means to ultimate fulfilment.

In Bali and Java, boys and girls marry as young as 14, celebrating their union with feasts and music. Arranged marriages are rare and divorce is almost non-existent. Women, although subservient to their husbands, do have an element of independence.

In the rural villages and towns, where the majority of Indonesians live, the extended family remains the heart of traditional society. Around the house uncles, aunts, brothers and sisters generally live as one unit, eating, working

Religious festivals form an important part of everyday life in Bali

Ancient stone reliefs at Borobudur educate Buddhist pilgrims

and sleeping together. And when the parents are old, it is the duty of the children to provide financial and spiritual support.

Indeed, with the support from family and religion, Indonesians suffer little of the isolation felt by many of their more progressive neighbours, relying on the gods and the community to help them through the ups and downs of everyday life.

The Arts

Art is one of the greatest expressions of the sheer *joie de vivre* of the people of Indonesia. It is reflected in the finely carved temples and palaces, the intricate wooden carvings, batiks and colourful paintings. Even the *gamelan* orchestra and the epic Ramayana dance are performed in many towns and villages throughout Bali and Java.

Originally these arts strictly adhered to religious or royal lines. These days they have increasingly been influenced by Western artistry and by more individual interpretations of traditional themes. The result is a sparkling mixture of colour and style that has become one of Indonesia's most celebrated gifts to the world.

Politics

*F*or a country consisting of so many scattered islands and with such ethnic diversity, Indonesia's recent politics have shown remarkable stability – if a poor human rights record. Since 1968, the country has been ruled by one president. It has a people's consultative assembly made up of 1,000 members, a constitution and elections are held every five years. Furthermore, at grass-roots level, the republic consists of 27 provinces, each of which is headed by a governor appointed for a five-year term.

The political status quo has created in Indonesia one of the few developing countries where conflicts have been minimal and where elements of national cohesion are evident. But under President Suharto, now undergoing his sixth term in power, Indonesia has long been ruled with an iron hand.

Currently there are only three legal political parties, namely the ruling Golkar party which includes all state employees in its ranks, the Muslim-backed United Development Party and the Indonesian Democratic Party. Each of these parties is restricted in the extent of their opposition.

But while President Suharto has plenty of critics, even the most vocal opponents have been forced to applaud his success in holding together this far-flung archipelago as a united nation while presiding over one of the fastest growing economies in the Asian Pacific region. Over the last five years alone, Indonesia has established itself as a key member of the ASEAN (Association of Southeast Asian Nations) group of countries and an increasingly active participant in regional affairs. By the year 2019, President Suharto has even set the goal of achieving the status of a developed nation. Not such a wild target when you consider the rich diversity of Indonesia's natural resources.

Indeed, the biggest political questions now are who will succeed the sexagenarian, and how will any new president or military-backed government adapt to calls for growing political independence?

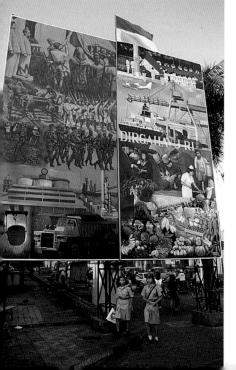

Government poster extolling the virtues of Freedom, Independence and National Unity

FIRST STEPS

'It was a sunrise such as we had
seldom seen, even though here in
the East they are so often almost
terrible in their loveliness.'

JAN POORTENAAR

An Artist in Java (1928)

INTRODUCTION

If you are arriving in Indonesia for the first time, there is no need to panic. Indonesia may be 11,263km from Europe, but it has plenty of comforts to add to its other charms. On Bali there are hotels to match any in the world, as well as all the usual facilities you would expect to find in a city. These days, even the telephones work in Jakarta – mostly. And while cultural and linguistic barriers may throw up a host of new challenges, they will also provide corresponding rewards. Below are a few hints to help you on your way.

AVOIDING OFFENCE

Indonesians have grace, humour and

Bamboo-caged songbirds are a ubiquitous sight throughout Southeast Asia and form an inherent part of Indonesian culture

BARE ESSENTIALS

Lost? Needing directions? Here are a few essential words to help you on your way.

Kamar Kecil Toilet
Bemo Motorised jeep
Becak Tricycle with passenger seats
Bukit Hill
Gunung Mountain
Istanana Palace
Jalan Street
Kali Canal
Merdan Square
Pasar Market
Polisi Police
Stanplatz Bus or taxi station
Stasiun keretapi Train station
Tolong Help

poise in abundance, along with plenty of sensitivities. To avoid causing offence, never touch anyone on the head or point your finger at them; when passing food or shaking hands, always remember to use your right hand, since the left is generally used for bodily ablutions; never insult a religion or make offensive comments about the country's politics, and avoid public displays of affection, which will reduce most locals to uncontrollable fits of laughter. Finally, always treat people with the respect they deserve. Doing so will make your life and theirs immeasurably more pleasant.

BARGAINING

Forget the notion of fixed prices while in Indonesia. You will find that almost everywhere, apart from in hotels and supermarkets, bargaining is the norm and to perfect this art needs neither guile nor aggression, just a little common sense and a lot of humour. First ask the price of an article, then name a figure considerably lower and somewhat less than the amount you want to pay, and eventually agree on a compromise. If neither party can agree, no damage is done, and it's simply a question of moving on and starting the process all over again.

COPING WITH THE HEAT

When you first arrive in Indonesia the heat will hit you quite forcibly. Whether it be May or November, it is likely to be hot, or if not hot, then wet, and if you come at the wrong time, both. To cope with the heat, allow time to acclimatise, take hats and sun-tan lotion and consume large quantities of bottled water. If you are concerned about your state of health or your ability to cope with the heat, see a doctor before you leave. Don't spend too long in the sun for the first few days – severe sunburn will not only leave you looking like a lobster, but may spoil the remainder of your holiday.

CULTURE SHOCK

In practice culture shock is more a state of mind than a physical debilitation. To cope with it, simply relax, put your preconceptions aside and enjoy the novelty of any given situation. The fact that some people may dine on barbecued dog flavoured with grated coconut in no way reflects any moral inferiority, and although some norms of behaviour may be hard to stomach, always try to reserve judgement. When you return home take careful note of your own country's shortcomings – you may be a little more tolerant.

GREETINGS

Saying *selamat pagi* to an Indonesian is like saying 'good morning' to an Englishman, and everyone will appreciate it. Those with a more advanced linguistic repertoire can show greater refinement. If it's between noon and 3pm, say *selamat siang* (good afternoon); between 3pm and 6pm opt for *selamat sore* (good evening); and between 6pm and midnight, wish people *selamat malam* (good night). Making an effort in this way will not only earn you respect, but occasionally even an invitation to someone's home. Only businessmen need shake hands, although obviously if someone holds their hand out it would be churlish not to respond.

HASSLES

Everyone is likely to be subjected to hassle at some stage during their holiday and the cause may be anything from disagreement over the price of a lurid wooden elephant to a tout becoming angry or a policeman wanting 'baksheesh'. Whatever you do, don't lose your temper as this is greatly frowned upon. If an official wants a bribe, smile and feign ignorance. If someone follows you around in the hope of becoming your tour guide, thank him for his interest, but make it clear that you would prefer to go without. Finally, relax and smile, as this will always prove your most potent weapon. When it comes to theft you should simply leave and report the incident to a higher authority. But take the locals on yourself? Never.

HOSPITALITY

With more than 100,000 temples and mosques and countless gods looking after them, it is little wonder that Indonesians can afford to be happy and hospitable. Don't necessarily expect to find them that way in all the major tourist centres.

Islamic tradition encourages women to cover up in public

Welcome to Indonesia, with a touch of charm

Often the people in these places have got used to the rudities and strangeness of tourists. Outside, however, Indonesians are some of the most delightful people in the world. Often you may be approached by locals just wanting to find out where you come from, and sometimes they may invite you to their homes. For the most part these are acts of friendliness, but always beware as, although most Indonesians have hearts of gold, somewhere along the line you may meet the exception.

INDONESIAN TALK

Visitors wanting to converse with all 185 million inhabitants in Indonesia may have to learn 300 different languages. Less ambitious mortals can limit themselves to just one: Bahasa Indonesia. This national language, based on Bahasa Malaysia, is relatively easy to pick up and has no complicated tenses, genders or articles. On top of that you may also come across Sundanese, Betawi Madurese and Javanese, as well as Dutch and Chinese dialects and occasionally even English. For a handful of basic words and phrases, see pages 182–3. For a greater choice of vocabulary, buy a dictionary or study a language course before you depart.

'Jam Karet'

The Indonesians have a wonderful phrase for 'late'. It is called *Jam Karet*, or rubber time, and in practice it governs everything from train departures to business meetings and even delivery of your breakfast. Before you despair, however, remember that although in the West time is money, in Indonesia time is still a quality to be valued and enjoyed. So if you find yourself having to wait for any length of time, take a deep breath, smell the sweet-scented blossoms, look at the shrines with their offerings for the gods and contain your anger – at least until later.

LAND OF GODS

When on Bali or Lombok, keep an eye out for the small spirit houses or shrines which are built to honour the spirits, the most important inhabitants on the island. These entities live in the trees, in the winds and the rains. If treated with respect, they ensure plentiful rice harvests, good health and happiness. But if overlooked, they will cause drought, death and a thousand traumas. To ensure harmony, good spirits must be thanked with offerings and colourful festivities, and bad spirits appeased by gifts of rice and joss sticks placed on the ground every morning.

AND SPIRITS

Nor is it only the spirits that must be honoured. In every village you will find countless temples and shrines dedicated to the gods Brahma, Shiva and Vishnu, as well as temples for the dead and temples for the founding of the village – indeed, there are so many places of worship that it is little wonder that the island remains an earthly paradise.

There are plenty of temples on Java, too, from the magnificent Buddhist temple of Borobudur to the fine Hindu *candis* at nearby Prambanan and Dieng Plateau. Added to those are statues of the elephant-headed Ganesha and of Kartteya, the six-headed god of war. These days, the island plays host to some 50,000 mosques where more than 80 per cent of the population come to pray, many of them doing so up to five times a day to give thanks to Allah (the prophet Mohammed).

Just to make sure that nobody's been overlooked on Java, Bali or Lombok, there are even holy trout

swimming around in the temple lakes, fed with peanuts and protected by joss sticks and holy water. Religion? In Indonesia it's almost a way of life.

Top, far left: Balinese shrine
Left and above: Borobudur
Top, right: Balinese temple carvings, Ubud

The famous palace of Kertha Gosa in Klungkung, on the island of Bali

A MATTER OF FACE

Maintaining face in Indonesia is as important as wearing underclothes in Europe and those who find themselves deprived of this important commodity tend to lash out accordingly. To avoid undue insult, always pay due respect to senior officials and to members of established families. Never criticise a manager in front of his employees or disagree with a father in front of his children. Remember, too, that the most important person should always stand tallest, which is why you often see the locals desperately craning their necks forward to keep their heads at a low level. While most Indonesians do not expect foreigners to behave in exactly the same way, they will appreciate your deference to their sensitivities.

SAFETY

Petty theft and pick-pocketing may be one of Indonesia's biggest growth industries, but it is certainly no worse than in many other countries. To reduce risks, take a few simple precautions. Buy a money belt in which to place cash and passports, and carry photocopies with details of passport number, air tickets, travellers' cheques and insurance separately. Always check to see that your hotel room is secure and leave valuables in the hotel safe. Beware public buses and trains where robberies are most common. Above all, try not to put temptation in the way of people. A camera may cost just US$200, but to a poor labourer it's worth more than a year's wages for working in the rice fields.

STRAIGHT TALK
Ask five Indonesians the way to the bus stop and you'll probably get five different answers. It's not that they lie or mislead deliberately, but are simply too proud to admit that they don't know. To avoid this problem, ask someone at your hotel to write down directions and take a map.

TEMPLES AND MOSQUES
Whether it is a temple, a spirit house or a mosque filled with prostrate Muslims, treat it as you would any other house of worship. Before entering a Balinese temple, tie a sash around your waist and leave a small donation (generally Rp1,000). Most temples forbid women from entering while they are in menstruation as it is considered unclean; some even forbid women who are pregnant, or insane. On Java and Lombok everyone can enter a mosque, but always observe the appropriate customs. Remove your shoes before entering and wash your feet in the facilities provided. Women especially should dress conservatively and avoid shorts, singlets or short skirts.

WHAT TO WEAR
There is no need to take thick woollen clothes or anything made from synthetic material unless you are heading up into the hills. Better to stock up on cotton shorts and open shirts, skirts and blouses and a large hat to protect you from the sun. T-shirts, sarongs and shorts can be bought in abundance in many of the tourist areas. If you are staying in a smart hotel, take more formal wear for evening dinner. Only for official calls and formal occasions are a jacket and tie or dresses and blouses a pre-requisite.

Party wear, Balinese style

WHAT'S A CANDI?
The Javanese refer to them as *candi* and the Balinese as *pura*, but to most people they are simply temples. You may come across other confusing terms too. A *stupa* is a Buddhist tower, normally in the shape of a bell and a *mandala* is an elaborate geometric figure used for meditation. Finally the term you are most likely to hear is 'cosmic mountain', which refers to Mount Meru, seat of the gods.

Every village in Bali holds a temple ceremony at least once a year

and, near by, Ujung Kulon National Park, one of the last remaining strongholds of the Java rhinoceros.

Central Java

You will find an abundance of temples, volcanoes and pleasant mountain retreats within easy reach of popular Yogyakarta and Surakarta (Solo). There is plenty of culture here too, from beautiful batiks to shadow puppets, as well as wild coastal seas at Parangtritis.

East Java

Although East Java is the least developed region on the island, visitors will be rewarded with some of the most diverse scenery, ranging from magnificent Mount Bromo to the rarely visited Baluran National Park, and the arid island of Madura, still barely established on the tourist map.

Bali

Surfers flock to Bali, one of the world's most beautiful islands. Alternatively, there are beaches and tranquillity in up-market Sanur or Nusa Dua, as well as temples, festivals and exotic scenery in the countryside beyond. For the perfect getaway, visit Ubud, cultural centre and stepping-stone to the countless villages dotted around the heartlands.

Lombok

Lombok offers many of the attractions of Bali, but without the crowds. For sun, sand and sea, relax on Senggigi Beach or the idyllic Gili islands; for something more energetic, climb Gunung Rinjani, the highest volcano on the island.

EXPLORING JAVA, BALI AND LOMBOK

Once you have got your feet firmly on Indonesian soil, the next step is to organise your itinerary. A glittering choice of attractions awaits you, but don't make the mistake of trying to see everything in one go. It is better to get to know one area well than to rush from one site to another, taking in almost nothing.

Jakarta

Although many people take an instant dislike to this bustling metropolis of 8 million people, Jakarta does have plenty of attractions as well as fine restaurants, nightclubs and five-star accommodation.

West Java

West Java may not play host to many tourists, but it does offer hill resorts, tea plantations and tropical islands. In the far west you will find Krakatau, one of the world's most destructive volcanoes

WHAT TO SEE

'In the whole course of my life, I have never met with such stupendous and finished specimens of human labour.'

CAPTAIN GEORGE BAKER

1810

Java

One of the lushest, most heavily populated and diverse islands on earth, Java literally bristles with colour and fascination. It is an area of beautiful mountains, tea plantations and unspoilt beaches. It is also home to magnificent temples, fertile rice fields – and some very dirty and crowded cities.

Although Java covers only 6 per cent of the country's land mass, it contains 60 per cent of the population with the result that some 110 million people live in one of the most concentrated and crowded areas of the world. Jakarta, the capital, boasts some 8 million of these people, along with more than its fair share of cars, high-rise buildings and slums.

Yet a 2-hour drive to the south of Jakarta will bring you to the unhurried cool of a mountain resort or the famous botanical gardens of Bogor. Take a regular speed boat from Ancol Marina, and you could even find yourself sunbathing on an exotic tropical island surrounded by turquoise seas.

Java also has ancient temples influenced by the great religions of Buddhism and Hinduism which dominated this country before Islam took hold. In addition to Borobudur and Prambanan, there are a host of other lesser-known temples and palaces. Afterwards, you can visit the volcanoes at Mount Meru, Krakatau or Mount Bromo or just wander through the forests in one of the island's national parks.

On returning to the major towns a different world awaits you: a world of factories, busy ports and warehouses, along with endless plantations and the fertile rice fields which produce up to three crops a year. Java is also the administrative centre for Indonesia's sprawling island archipelago and the

JAVA

The beautifully tranquil botanical gardens at Cibodas in West Java

country's economic powerhouse, generating more than 80 per cent of the nation's wealth.

Most people stay on Java for just a few days to acquire a taste of the place, then continue on to Bali and Lombok; however, anyone who opts for a longer stay will be richly rewarded.

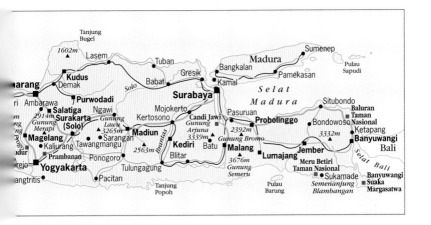

Jakarta

*I*f Indonesia's sprawling capital is your first stop, be prepared for heat, chaos and some of the most interminable traffic jams on earth. Many people take an instant dislike to this bustling metropolis of 8 million people, complaining of the pollution, the poverty and the sheer magnitude of the city. But for those who have the time and the inclination there is plenty of history, culture and even fun to be found, although you may have to search for it.

Founded in the 16th century as a small trading port at the mouth of the Ciliwung River, Jakarta – or Batavia as it was later known – was razed by the Dutch in 1619 and rebuilt as the capital of the Dutch East Indies, sporting canals, grandiose squares and red-tiled houses.

Those somnolent days have long since passed, however, and since independence in 1949 the city has played host not only to the president, but to increasing numbers of high-rise blocks, five-star hotels and glitzy nightclubs.

Don't be put off, though, by these trappings of modernity. Outside the centre Jakarta remains a fascinating city of labyrinthine side streets and crowded markets with plenty to see and do. Around the town you will discover a mind-boggling variety of culinary specialities, as well as shops and bazaars

with a huge collection of arts and crafts from all over the country. Indeed, whilst Jakarta is certainly not the city of the gods, it does offer subtle rewards to those who make the effort.

Getting Around

To avoid the ubiquitous traffic jams avoid travelling between 8am and 10am or 5pm and 7pm and to negotiate the one-way streets, overpasses and twisting side streets, take a taxi. If you need a landmark, look for the soaring National Monument in Medan Merdeka which is in the heart of town. To miss the traffic altogether, tour the city on a Sunday.

GLODOK (Chinatown)

For a glimpse of old Chinatown visit the colourful market on Jalan Pancoran, which is intersected by little alleyways and wooden houses. The Chinese moved to this district in 1741 following a massacre and have been making money there ever since. Explore the back streets where you will find little temples and a host of stalls selling glutinous noodle dishes and occasionally even shark's fin soup. Near the Glodok City Hotel, the less adventurous can settle for grapes and apples, or beautiful flowers.
Jalan Pancoran is situated off Jalan Pintu Besar in the north of the city.

Jalan Pancoran, Chinatown

ISTANA MERDEKA (Freedom Palace)

This splendid palace was built in 1879 to house the Dutch governors and although the official residence of the president it is now only used on state occasions. At the front of the building is a large portico with Corinthian pillars and the first room, behind the terrace, is the Credential Hall where the president accepts letters from foreign ambassadors. *Northwest corner of Medan Merdeka. Closed to the public.*

JALAN JENDRAL SUDIRMAN/ JALAN THAMRIN

This main road which changes its name from Jalan Thamrin to Jalan Jendral Sudirman is Jakarta's equivalent of New York's Wall Street, London's Mayfair and Paris's Champs-Elysées rolled into one. It hosts countless banks, insurance companies, shopping centres and the new Grand Hyatt Hotel, the city's biggest showpiece in luxury accommodation.

Rush hour on Jalan Jendral Sudirman

JAKARTA

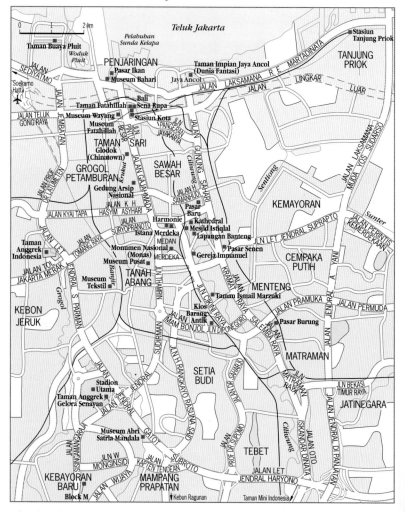

KEBUN RAGUNAN (Ragunan Zoo)

At weekends, thousands of locals invade Indonesia's biggest zoo. Visitors with an interest in wildlife can watch the orangutans, crocodiles and the famous Komodo dragons, as well as visit a new breeding enclosure for the rare Sumatran tigers. To avoid the crowds, go during the week.

14km south of Jakarta in Ragunan, near

From statues of welcome to concrete columns, Jakarta is littered with monuments

Pasar Minggu. Buses run direct from the centre of town. Open: daily, 8am–6pm. Admission charge.

KIOS BARANG ANTIK

Jakarta's famous flea market is worth a visit for the fun of it, but you may not find much of any real value here. The choice of goods is vast, ranging from brass chandeliers to plastic suitcases. Treat any claims as to age or authenticity with a certain amount of scepticism.
Jalan Surabaya, in Menteng district, to the south of Medan Merdeka. Open: daily, 9am–5pm. Admission free.

A DEADLY CHARM

Jakarta's reputation of being thoroughly unhealthy has more than a little substance. During the 17th century its position on swampland meant it was one of the most disease-ridden cities in the East. Indeed, when Captain Cook put into Jayakarta half his crew died of malaria.

MEDAN MERDEKA (Freedom Square)

You won't be able to miss this giant public square which claims to be one of the largest of its kind in the world. Years ago it was a military parade ground, but now it is a huge park containing state headquarters, the National Monument, the modern parliament building, the national museum and the state palace.
Central Jakarta. Occupies the area between Jalan Thamrin and Jalan Menteng Raya.

MESJID ISTIQLAL (Istiqlal Mosque)

The Istiqlal mosque took more than 10 years to build and is reputed to be the second largest mosque in Southeast Asia, as well as one of the largest in the world. Close up, the edifice is awesome with its six levels, its minarets and its enormous white dome. Visit the mosque on Fridays to see it filled with capacity crowds of up to 200,000, but remember to dress suitably.
Jalan Veteran. Off the northeast corner of Medan Merdeka. Admission free.

COLONIAL ARCHITECTURE

In parts of Java, Dutch architecture is almost as abundant as tulips in spring. It is found in the beautiful old façades that front the narrow alleyways of old Batavia, and in the austere courts of justice and magnificent squares that are scattered around the Kota district. Even murky canals still wind their way through labyrinths of closely packed houses and mounds of garbage.

Of course plenty of the old buildings have been knocked down and replaced by faceless new shopfronts and modern houses, but you'll still find reminders of the days when the Dutch sailed their boats into the harbour and commandeered much of the surrounding archipelago.

In Jakarta's old district of Sunda Kelapa, where the Dutch fort still stands, you could almost be in a European capital with its old warehouses, its Grecian-style museum and distinguished European edifices. Hardly surprising, then, that during the early days the town was known as 'Little Amsterdam'. In Surabaya, Yogyakarta, and Malang – and even high up in the hill resorts – you can still find glimpses of the days when the colonial administrators retreated from the heat of the plains below.

To the interiors of their great buildings the Dutch added fine statues, stained-glass windows and portraits to remind them of home and at night they held great parties with orchestras; the women wore long dresses and the men sported dinner jackets and stiff white collars.

This era ended in 1949, however, and the Dutch, along with their suits and their parasols, departed, leaving behind them an independent Indonesia.

Left: the Mangkunegaran
Palace, Surakarta
Far left: the Bank Indonesia
building, Yogyakarta
Below: the Museum
Fatahillah, Jakarta
Bottom: detail from the
Surakarta Kraton

The National Monument is Jakarta's most prominent landmark

MONUMEN NASIONAL (National Monument)

Towering over the central part of Jakarta and referred to surreptitiously as 'Soekarno's last erection', this vast monument has almost everything except artistic merit. Built out of Italian marble and rising 137m, it was begun in 1961 to commemorate Indonesia's struggle for independence and is topped by a symbolic flame of freedom covered with 35kg of pure gold leaf. For the best photographs, take the elevator up to the platform. Afterwards, visit the museum below and listen to the voice of former President Soekarno broadcasting the declaration of independence.
Medan Merdeka (tel: 340 452). Open: daily, 8.30am–5pm. Admission charge.

MUSEUM FATAHILLAH (City Museum)

This fine two-storey building is one of the best examples of Dutch colonial architecture that you are likely to come across in Jakarta. Built in 1710, it became a museum in 1974 and now provides exhibits of Dutch colonial life as well as an insight into the city's 350-year history. From the first-floor balcony you can look down on the square where criminals were executed or severely flogged (see Kota II walk, pages 42–3). *Corner of Taman Fatahillah, across the road from the Wayang Museum. Tel: 679 101. Open: Tuesday to Thursday, 8am–2pm; Friday, 8am–11am; Saturday, 8am–1pm; Sunday, 8am–2pm. Admission charge.*

This distinguished building houses the delightful Museum Fatahillah

MUSEUM PUSAT (National Museum)

Established in 1778 under the auspices of the Batavia Association of Arts and Sciences, this museum has so much to offer that you may find yourself overwhelmed. Allow plenty of time and take a camera, although you must first obtain a permit at the entrance. Some of the most interesting exhibits are to be found in the prehistory section which contains weapons and cooking utensils,

Jakarta's popular Pasar Burung has more than raucous roosters

as well as a skull of the 'Java Man', discovered in the 1890s in East Java and hailed as the 'missing link' between apes and humans. There is also a fine display of pottery and Oriental porcelain as well as treasure rooms, inner courts and an audio-visual room. Conducted tours in English are held on Tuesday, Wednesday and Thursday mornings at 9.30am and last for around 2.5 hours.

Jalan Merdeka Barat 12, on the west side of Medan Merdeka (tel: 360 551). Open: Tuesday to Thursday, 8am–2pm; Fridays, 8am–11am; Saturday, 11am–1pm; Sundays, 8am– 2pm. Closed Mondays. Admission charge.

MUSEUM TEKSTIL (Textile Museum)

Textile enthusiasts should not miss this museum housed in a 19th-century residence to the southwest of town. The collection contains just about every kind of fabric from the most far-flung areas of the archipelago.

Jalan Satsuit Tuban 4 (tel: 365 367).

Open: Tuesday to Thursday, and Sunday, 8am–2pm; Friday, 8am–11am; Saturday, 8am–1pm. Admission charge.

PASAR BURUNG (Bird Market)

This market is the place to view *perkutut* song birds as well as colourful parrots and occasionally even the helmeted hornbill. These creatures are piled up in bamboo cages along with roosters and, sadly, rarer breeds that have escaped the eye of conservationists.

A short distance down Jalan Pramuka, in Jatinegara. Open: daily, 9am–5pm. Admission free.

PASAR IKAN (Fish Market)

The old fish market with its auction rooms and colourful stalls occupies an area of narrow alleyways in the old part of town next to the harbour of Sunda Kelapa. Get there early in the morning to see the place at its liveliest (see Kota I walk, pages 40–1).

Pasar Ikan Road, north of Taman Fatahillah. Open: daily.

Old Buginese Makassar schooners still sail the seas with cargos of spices

SUNDA KELAPA

If you only have time to visit one place in Jakarta, choose the magnificent harbour in the old part of town – but allow plenty of time because of the appalling traffic. All along the wharf, which is spread out beside the stinking Ciliwung River, beautiful old Buginese Makassar schooners are loaded up with timber, cartons of Coca Cola and other local commodities destined for the outer islands. For a small fee you can take a short trip around the harbour in a rowing boat, but beware the ropes – and the

MONUMENTAL TASTELESSNESS

From bronze statues to concrete columns and knights charging into battle, Jakarta is littered with monuments to athletes, to the army and even to farmers. Not all have won accolades. The statue of Welcome is nicknamed 'Hansel and Gretel', whilst the famous gentleman holding a flaming dish is simply called 'the mad waiter'.

A mouthful of monuments at Mini-Indonesia

slops which are merrily thrown overboard (see Kota I walk, pages 40–1).
Jalan Krapu, in the north of the city, a short distance from Pasar Ikan. Open: daily, 8am–6pm. Admission charge.

TAMAN IMPIAN JAYA ANCOL

This vast Western-style amusement park is a must for children and fun-loving adults. There's an oceanarium, a multi-million dollar swimming pool complex with wave-making facilities, as well as bowling alleys, space shuttles, jumping dolphins and even kissing seals. Go during the week for peace and quiet.
2km north of Jakarta at Ancol (tel: 681 511). Bus no 64 runs from Kota Station. Open: Monday to Friday, 3pm–10pm; Saturday and Sunday, 10am–10pm. Admission charge.

TAMAN ISMAIL MARZUKI

Before dropping by this municipal arts centre, obtain a list of performances from your hotel or the English-language newspapers. Cultural entertainment ranges from Javanese dancing to *gamelan* concerts and batik exhibitions.
Jalan Cikini Raya (tel: 337 530). Open: Monday to Saturday, 9am–1pm. Admission charge.

TAMAN MINI-INDONESIA

Visitors wanting to see the great monuments of Indonesia – with minimum effort – can simply go to the Taman Mini-Indonesia, now billed as Jakarta's top tourist attraction. Among the dazzling number of exhibits spread over 120 hectares are finely crafted houses from each of the 27 provinces of Indonesia, models of the country's major landmarks, as well as theatres, boating lakes, trams, cable-cars and a miniature train. You will find a history museum, acclaimed as the country's best, as well as a wildlife and natural history museum located inside the statue of a Komodo dragon which towers 25m above the ground. There is also an orchid garden containing more than 2,000 varieties of orchid. You would need weeks to see all the sights, but even a day's visit will provide you with a memorable introduction.
20km south of Jakarta, just off the toll expressway to Bogor (tel: 801 905). Take a bus to Cililitan, then change to a 'mini-Indonesia' bus or, better still, take a tour. Open: daily, 9am–4pm. Admission charge.

WAYANG MUSEUM, see Kota II walk, pages 42–3.

Jakarta

JAVA · Surabaya
Yogyakarta · Surakarta

Kota I

Starting at the delightful old port of Sunda Kelapa, this walk will take you through an area known as 'Little Amsterdam'. It is made up of fetid canals, old Dutch warehouses, European-style bridges and colourful markets. *Allow 3 hours.*

Get up at dawn to avoid the traffic and take a bus or taxi to the entrance of Sunda Kelapa which lies to the north of the city in the old Kota district.

1 SUNDA KELAPA

Centuries ago, this magnificent wharf was Jakarta's only major link with the outside world. These days it is still the departure point for ancient vessels laden with sugar and spices and you can watch the old Bugis schooners with their towering wooden masts being loaded up for their next voyage. For a small sum you can take a rowing boat around the harbour.
Return to the entrance gate and continue for 200m. Turn right over the bridge on to Jalan Pakin and you will see the Uitkijk.

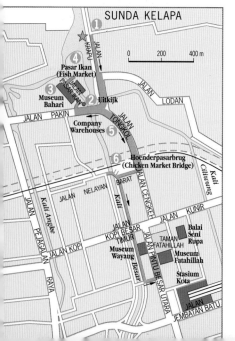

2 UITKIJK (LOOK-OUT TOWER)

Built by the Dutch in 1839, this old look-out tower was used both to signal to incoming ships and as a vantage point. Climb up to the top for excellent photo opportunities. Note, too, the cannons pointing towards Sunda Kelapa.
Turn right down Jalan Pasar Ikan and almost immediately you will see the Museum Bahari on your left.

3 MUSEUM BAHARI

These two old warehouses were originally used to store tea, coffee, tin and spices. These days they have not only been restored, but transformed into a maritime museum with models of various fishing boats and other navigational items. In front of the museum are the last remnants of the wall which surrounded old Batavia in the 17th and 18th centuries.
Continue down Jalan Pasar Ikan until you

*reach the fish market, a short distance
further on.*

4 PASAR IKAN (FISH MARKET)

The time to see this fish market is at dawn
when piles of freshly caught barramundi
and tuna line the stalls and the auction
halls are crowded with buyers. You can
explore the maze of small alleyways which
run parallel with the waterfront and buy
exotic fruits, clothes, hardware or
delicious *nasi goreng* (fried rice).
*Retrace your steps over the bridge and turn
right down Jalan Tongkol. After a few
hundred metres you will see the old
warehouses on your right.*

5 COMPANY WAREHOUSES

These dilapidated 19th-century
warehouses with their corrugated roofs
and flag poles were used to store grain and
spices. The area is now mainly used as a

car park, although you may see the odd
goat nibbling on grass near the entrance.
*Continue along Jalan Tongkol until you
reach the main intersection with Jalan
Nelayan Barat. Turn right and on your right
you will see the Hoenderpasarbrug.*

6 HOENDERPASARBRUG (CHICKEN MARKET BRIDGE)

This charming red-painted drawbridge
which crosses the Kali Besar Canal was
built in the 17th century and marks the
southwest corner of the old Dutch fort. It
is also the last of its kind in the city, and a
reminder of the days when boats used to
sail all the way up to Ciliwung River. On
the nearby road bridge you may find a
small market where you can refresh
yourself with cool drinks, and
occasionally even a slice of *durian*.
*Continue south parallel to the Kali Besar,
past some run-down old colonial buildings. At
the second junction, turn left and left again
on to Jalan Pintu Besar Utara where you
will find Taman Fatahillah (Fatahillah
Square; see Kota II walk, pages 42–3).
Alternatively, catch a taxi back to your hotel.*

Shopping at Pasar Ikan

Kota II: Fatahillah Square

Starting out in the heart of the old Dutch city, this walk takes you to some of the finest museums in Jakarta. You can explore the old square before taking a short walk past the Bank of Indonesia to the Portuguese Sion Church. *Allow 2.5 hours.*

Catch a bus or taxi to Taman Fatahillah, which lies in the Kota district, a short distance south of Sunda Kelapa.

1 TAMAN FATAHILLAH

Although this square has been extensively renovated, it still gives a delightful sense of Batavia's past with its old colonial buildings, its fountains and nearby canals. The square was built in the 17th century and designed by the Dutch Governor-General, Jan Pieterzoon Coen.
Standing in the centre of Taman Fatahillah, the Museum Fatahillah is directly in front.

2 MUSEUM FATAHILLAH

This distinguished old building, which dominates the square, was at various times both a military headquarters and the city hall. Inside the museum is a fine selection of Dutch memorabilia ranging from antique furniture to busts and portraits of former governors. Outside, you can explore the dungeons now filled with old cannon balls. (See also page 36.)
Leave the Museum Fatahillah and a short distance to your right you will see the Balai Seni Rupa.

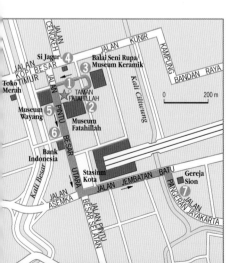

3 BALAI SENI RUPA (FINE ARTS MUSEUM)

Formerly the palace of justice, this fine little museum, built in the 1870s, now plays host to famous paintings by prominent Indonesian artists such as

Raden Saleh, as well as to a selection of ceramics, terracotta and Javanese water jugs. Note, too, the rare Ming pieces gathered together by Adam Malik.
From the Fine Arts Museum, cross back into the square and on your right you will see a large bronze cannon.

4 SRI JAGUR

Legend tells that this bronze cannon was brought to Batavia in 1641 by the Dutch after the fall of Malacca. These days, it has established itself as the city's pre-eminent fertility symbol and you may occasionally see women sitting astride the cannon in the hope of conceiving children. Behind the cannon is a lively market selling clothes, fruits and other items.
Leave the square and cross over on to Jalan Pintu Besar Utara. Turn left and the Museum Wayang is on your right.

5 MUSEUM WAYANG

This two-storey building, which originally served as the museum of Old Batavia, now contains a collection of puppets from all over the world, including magnificent Chinese hand-puppets and the intricate buffalo-hide shadow puppets known as Wayang Kulit.
Walk out of the museum and turn right down Jalan Pintu Besar Utara. After a short distance the Bank Indonesia is passed on the right.

6 BANK INDONESIA

This grand-looking edifice houses one of the most important financial institutions in the country. The Bank of Indonesia, which is the country's central bank, sets the exchange rate, monitors the 160 different banking companies and advises the government on economic policy.

OPENING DETAILS
Museum Fatahillah. See page 36.
Balai Seni Rupa (tel: 676 090).
Open: Tuesday to Thursday,
8am–2pm; Friday, 8am–11am;
Saturday and Sunday, 8am–1pm;
closed Monday.
Museum Wayang (tel: 679 560).
Open:.Tuesday to Thursday, and
Sunday, 8am–2pm; Friday,
8am–11am; Saturday, 8am–1pm.

From Bank Indonesia, continue until you reach the main square in front of the station. Turn left on to Jalan Jembatan Batu and then third right to Gereja Sion.

7 GEREJA SION (SION CHURCH)

This incongruous little church, which dates from 1695, not only has a charming interior with copper chandeliers and a baroque pulpit, but is listed in the history books as the oldest church in Jakarta. It was originally built by the Portuguese, although it has since been renovated several times.
Catch a bus or taxi back to your hotel.

Fine leather shadow puppets are found throughout Indonesia's archipeligo

West Java

Stretching from the Selat Sunda (Sunda Straits) in the west to the border of Central Java, this province gives you a choice of lush rain forests, beautiful hill resorts, tea plantations and dazzling islands. Here you can rest amidst tropical splendour at the Pulau Seribu (Thousand Islands), visit the botanical gardens of Bogor or catch a boat out to Krakatau, one of the world's most destructive volcanoes. All these destinations can either make a perfect break from the bustle of Jakarta, or be used as stepping-stones on the way to Central Java and to Bali which lies further to the east.

BANDUNG

A 3-hour drive from the heat and hassle of Jakarta will bring you to Java's third largest city, situated on a plateau to the southeast. Bandung is the cultural centre of West Java, home to some of its best-known universities and to some of its most modern architecture. During the 1930s it was known as the Paris of Java, although these days you will find precious few noteworthy buildings and little reason to spend much time here. *Location: 180km southeast of Jakarta.*

Regular buses run from the Cililitan terminal on Jalan Jend Sutoyo (tel: 884 554). Trains depart from Jakarta Gambir, situated on Jalan Medan Merdeka Timur (tel: 342 777 or 352 981). Also served by Merpati flights.

Dago Hill Tea House

For the finest views that Bandung has to offer, visit this little tea house situated to

The overwhelming formality of Bandung's Gedung Sate

the north of the city, beyond the Sheraton Hotel. Get there at sunset to see the place at its best, but be prepared for the bar/restaurant to be closed.
Jalan Juanda, 6km north of town. Admission charge.

Gedung Merdeka
Unless you are particularly interested in the history of the non-aligned movement, there is little reason to visit this building which hosted the Afro-Asia conference in 1955. All that's on offer is a small museum and occasionally a film of the event.
Jalan Asia Africa. Open: Tuesday to Friday, 8am–1pm. Admission charge.

Gedung Sate
Bandung's most imposing building has everything from lush green lawns to well-clipped hedges. You can't go inside though, as these days it has become the province's main administrative and telecommunications centre.
Jalan Diponegoro, a short distance to the north of town. Closed to the public.

BOGOR
The name of Bogor is almost synonymous with botanical gardens and few visitors come to this hill town without visiting them. There are, however, several other sites to see, including the imposing presidential palace known as Istana Bogor and the Zoological Museum. To avoid the crowds, visit on a weekday.
Location: 60km south of Jakarta. Regular buses run from the Cililitan terminal on Jalan Jend Sutoyo. Trains take 90 minutes from Jakarta's Gambir Station on Jalan Medan Merdeka Timur.

Botanical Gardens
These magnificent gardens have not

Sir Stamford Raffles sowed the seeds for the Bogor Botanical Gardens

become one of West Java's finest showcases without good reason. In all they extend over 87 hectares, boasting more than 15,000 specimens of exotic native plants, trees and bushes along with lakes and shady walkways. The gardens were founded in 1817 by Sir Stamford Raffles, and were subsequently tended by the then Dutch Governor-General van der Capellan. Since then numerous other new species have been added, including African water lilies and the famous Rafflesia, which is claimed to be the biggest flower in the world.
The entrance to the gardens is on Jalan Empang, on the south side. Open: daily, 8am–4pm. Closed Friday between 11am and 1pm. Admission charge.

Zoological Museum
This little museum boasts more than 250,000 specimens of birds, reptiles, insects and mammals, as well as the last rhinoceros from Tasikmalaya – stuffed.
Jalan Empang. Next to the botanical gardens. Open: daily, 8am–4pm. Admission charge.

CIBODAS

Although the botanical gardens of Bogor are better known, this high-altitude extension is beautifully tranquil, set away from the crowds near the slopes of Gunung Gede and Gunung Pangrango. In all there are some 80 hectares of gardens, planted in 1889 and still sprouting prolifically. Most visitors simply take walks in the park or shop for tropical plants and dazzling flowers in the 'nurseries' that line the street outside. Those in search of more energetic recreation can climb nearby Mount Gede, a 10-hour hike there and back, with the help of a guide.

Location: situated off the main road from Bogor to Bandung, near the town of Cipanas. Ask to be dropped off by the bus and catch a bemo for the last 5km to Cibodas. To climb Mount Gede, first obtain a permit from the PHPA office next to the entrance to the botanical gardens.

KRAKATAU

The world's most active volcano in reality blew itself to smithereens just over a century ago, but in its place you will find its offspring, Anak Krakatau (son of Krakatau), which is gradually rising out of the sea. If you want to explore the volcano a boat can be hired from Labuhan or Carita for the 4–6-hour trip, but only when seas are low and conditions permit. A better and safer alternative is to take an organised tour. During the monsoon season, between November and March, high seas mean that trips can be extremely hazardous.

Location: 50km off the west coast of Java. Charter a boat from Labuhan, Anyer or Carita, or make arrangements at the Carita Krakatau Beach Hotel. Tours can

UP IN SMOKE

When Krakatau erupted on the morning of 27 August, 1883, the noise could be heard as far afield as Sri Lanka, Burma and Australia. Great piles of volcanic debris landed in Madagascar and tons of rocks were hurled more than 20km into the sky. In all, some 295 villages in West Java and South Lampung on Sumatra were destroyed and an estimated 36,000 people killed. These days only a small cone remains, known as Anak Krakatau; occasionally it rumbles, producing ash, smoke and a lot of fear.

also be organised through travel agents in Jakarta.

MERAK

There's precious little reason to visit this sprawling town unless you are catching the ferry to Sumatra. Boats take 1.5 hours to reach Bakauheni and 4 to 6 hours to Strengsem. Enquire at travel agents for current departure times.

Location: 140km west of Jakarta. Trains arrive and depart twice daily for Jakarta's Tanah Abang Railway Station on Jalan J Jati Baru. Regular buses take 3 hours from Jakarta's Kalideres Terminal.

PANGANDARAN

This gem of a little fishing village is rapidly becoming West Java's most popular resort area, offering fine beaches as well as access to the nearby nature reserve at Pananjung Pangandaran. Keen swimmers head out to the west side of the peninsula, but check on local conditions and beware of

Above: enjoy Pangandaran's fishermen, but beware its dangerous tides and currents
Right: take the pick of the catch at the morning market

dangerous currents which take their toll every year. A safer option is to walk to the headland reserve, reached by crossing the narrow isthmus. For a pleasant morning's hiking, hire a guide at the entrance. You are bound to catch sight of monkeys and deer and if you are lucky you may even find the rare Rafflesia lotus flower which smells like rotting garbage and resembles a bloated pink cabbage.

Location: 400km southeast of Jakarta. Buses run from Bandung, Jakarta or Yogyakarta to the town of Banjar, from where you must catch another bus or bemo. Crowded boats also leave in the morning from the town of Cilacap, taking 4 hours.

Tea plantations cover the rolling hills around Puncak Pass

PANTAI CARITA

This 3km sweep of sand lined with coconut groves is a popular weekend haunt of expatriates and Jakartans, who leave the city in swarms. There is reasonable accommodation here and on clear days fine views of the distant Krakatau can be had. For information on trips to the volcano, call in at the Carita Krakatau Beach Hotel. Otherwise, spend the time snorkelling, surfing or taking lazy strolls into the nearby paddy fields.
Location: 150km west of Jakarta. Regular buses run from Jakarta's Kalideres Terminal to Labuhan, from where you must take the short minibus ride. Avoid at weekends.

PULAU SERIBU (Thousand Islands)

Weary city dwellers flock to the beautiful islands known as Pulau Seribu, or Thousand Islands, to laze under palm trees, swim in clear turquoise water and relax in a perfect hideaway just 2 to 4

hours by boat from the capital. Many of the islands are surrounded by sparkling white beaches; others are better known for their coral. Only a handful of them, however, have been fully developed as tourist destinations. For bungalows and cottages try Pulau Putri and Pulau Pelangi, though you should book in advance. To avoid the crowds go during the week and remember to take a sun hat, sun-tan lotion and heaps of mosquito repellent.
Location: 70km from Jakarta's waterfront. Boats run from Ancol Dreamland Marina in the north of the city, leaving every morning at around 7am and taking between 2 and 4 hours. Make an advance booking if you intend to stay the night. Alternatively, contact Seribu Tours (tel: 348 533).

PUNCAK PASS

You could travel to beautiful Puncak Pass (2,900m) for the views alone. It sits

high up in the heart of the tea-growing area east of Bogor, offering magnificent vistas of the surrounding area. Stop by the Gunung Mas tea estates (3km to the west) for photographs of the workers picking tea leaves and stacking them in giant wicker baskets. Tours of the plantation can be arranged on arrival. Afterwards, for a touch of tropical splendour, continue to the botanical gardens at Cibodas (10km to the east).
Location: 25km southeast of Bogor, on the road to Bandung or Cianjur. Catch one of the regular buses and ask to be dropped off at Puncak Pass.

TANGKUBAN PRAHU
The popular Tangkuban Prahu cannot compare with the awesome scenery around Mount Bromo or Mount Batur on Bali, but it can provide a pleasant excursion from Bandung. Legend has it that the crater is part of a giant upturned boat that an eccentric young prince built after he fell in love with his own mother. Pleasant walks can be taken around the

main crater and to a series of 11 craters in the vicinity, which are signposted. For ease of transport, take a tour.
Location: 32km north of Bandung, near the village of Lembang. From the park entrance it is 6km to the crater. Admission charge.

UJUNG KULON NATIONAL PARK
Java's finest national park makes up for its lack of tourist facilities with the largest concentration of wildlife on the island. There are plenty of colourful birds, deer, wild ox and crocodiles; park officials even claim that 50 protected rhinoceros live in the vicinity. Unless you have sufficient time, it is best to take a tour organised in Carita or Labuhan since access is difficult and expensive (see Getting Away From it All, pages 140–1).
Location: southwestern tip of Java. Reached by a 6–8-hour boat trip from Labuhan, which is situated midway along the coast. You must obtain an entry permit and, ideally, a guide from the PHPA office at Labuhan.

The inner crater at Tangkuban Prahu

Central Java

Central Java, stretching from Pangandaran east to Tawangmangu, offers a dazzling choice of destinations from rugged beaches to cool hill resorts, volcanoes and some of the most magnificent ruins on earth. This is the cultural heart of Indonesia, home to the great cities of Yogyakarta and Surakarta (Solo). It is also the region where you will find the temples of Borobudur and Prambanan, and the awesome Mount Merapi, along with some of the most colourful batiks and shadow puppets in the country. Buses and trains connect major towns with East Java and West Java.

YOGYAKARTA

Almost everybody who visits Central Java will spend some time in Yogyakarta, for this vibrant metropolis of 500,000 people oozes with history, culture and sheer exuberance.

Founded by the rebel prince Mangkubumi in 1755 following the division of the kingdom of Mataram, the town became one of the most powerful Javanese states until it was sacked by the British in 1812. At the end of World War II the city once again rose to prominence as the rebel capital of the new republic of Indonesia in its struggle for independence from the Dutch.

Those efforts did not go unnoticed and in 1949 the city was granted status as a special region, and the only one on Java to retain a functioning sultanate.

Yogyakarta (better known as Yogya) has plenty of attractions. You can explore the ancient ruins of the Taman Sari or the Kraton in the morning, shop for shadow puppets or traditional batiks in the afternoon and afterwards take a delightful tricycle ride to the artists' quarter or to the colourful bird market.

When the city's spell is finally broken, there are trips to the magnificent temples of Borobudur and Prambanan which, although easily done in a day, deserve longer.

Location: 565km east of Jakarta. Trains take 10 hours from Jakarta's Kota Station on Jalan Station 1 (tel: 679 194). Buses take 12 hours from the Pulo Gadung Terminal on the corner of Jalan Perintis Kemerdekaan and Jalan Bekasi Timur Raya. Garuda, Merpati, Bouraq and Sempati offer air connections to Adisucipto Airport, 8km east of town.

A stone guard at Yogyakarta's Kraton

Yogyakarta prides itself for its role in achieving national independence

Kraton (Sultan's Palace)

Yogya's most popular tourist site may lack immediate charm, but it will certainly reward more than a passing visit. Founded in 1755 to house Yogyakarta's sultans, the area around the Kraton has become the veritable heart of the city, home to countless shops, markets and private residences.

Modelled on the cosmos, the palace has a symbolic value aimed at ensuring harmony between the court and the divine forces of the universe. Even the inner courtyards mirror the oceans which surround the cosmic mountain of the deities. The present Sultan, Hamengkubuwono X, lives here, waited upon by several hundred loyal retainers and worshipped by the people.

To view the centrepiece of the palace situated within the old walls visit the Bangsal Kencono (Golden Pavilion) with its four teak pillars and its peaked roof that represents Mount Meru. To the south you will also find two 14th-century *gamelan* orchestras. To round off the tour, drop into the nearby Museum Kereta Kraton on Jalan Rotowijayan with its royal brass gongs and horse-drawn carriages, the most impressive of which is the Kereta Kyai Garuda Yeksa, built in the Netherlands in 1861 out of 18-carat gold.

Enter from the west gate off Jalan Rotowijayan. Open: Saturday to Thursday, 8am–2pm; Friday, 8am–11am. Admission charge includes a guided tour. Gamelan *rehearsals held on Mondays and Wednesdays, 10am–noon.*

SHADOW PUPPETS

Made from leather, beautifully carved by hand and painted with gilt or even gold, the sacred Wayang Kulit puppets are not only some of Indonesia's greatest works of art, but also one of the country's most beloved forms of entertainment.

Dating back more than 1,000 years, these frail figures supported on posts of wood are seen as instruments of the gods, and the very symbols of the struggle between good and evil.

Typically, the puppets enact a host of different and often well-known stories. Some feature epic events from the Indian *Ramayana*, others heroic deeds or tales of ferocious battles between the gods and mortals. Often the age-old performances are spiced with local political and historical references, punctuated by comedy and accompanied by the sounds of a four-piece *gamelan* orchestra.

For up to 8 hours at a time the puppet master, known as the *dalang*, sits cross-legged behind a screen lit up by the flame of an ancient oil lamp. During the entire performance he alone manipulates the puppets, chanting in up to 50 different narrative voices and beating the tiny cymbal with his feet in a unique display of drama and passion. Only at the end of the show is there silence when the left side of the screen is empty and the power of good symbolically vanquishes the power of evil.

You may occasionally come across full-length versions of the Wayang Kulit, held at temple festivals or as part of a local celebration. Shorter versions are also held at tourist venues in Yogyakarta or Ubud. Elsewhere, you will find plenty of factories producing the beautiful hand-made puppets, reminders of the frailty of man who is little more than a puppet on the bigger stage of life.

(*WAYANG KULIT*)

Shadow puppets have passed on stories from one generation to the next in a region of the world where the written word was not available to the vast majority of the populace

Gambira Loka Zoo

One of the highlights of Yogya's zoo is the famous Komodo dragon which comes from the Lesser Sunda Islands and is reported to be the oldest living species of lizard, dating back almost 60 million years. There are plenty of other animals, too, as well as 22 hectares of garden, an orchid nursery and a children's park.

Jalan Gembira Loca, to the east of town, beyond Kali Gajah Wong. Open: daily, 8am–5pm. Admission charge.

Jalan Malioboro (Marlboro Street)

Yogya's most colourful shopping district has everything from leather and batik shops to underwear stalls presided over by dozens of grinning *becap* (tricycle) drivers. To get to Pasar Beringharjo, the city's largest covered market, continue to the southern end where the road changes its name to Jalan Jen A Yani. Otherwise just wander through the district, especially in the early evening when the shops do a roaring trade.

Painters' Colony

Aspiring batik makers took a liking to the area around Taman Sari years ago, transforming the network of little alleyways into a veritable batik painters' colony. Many of the older residents still specialise in traditional scenes from the *Ramayana*, but others have opted for a more surrealist style aimed at pleasing the growing Western clientele. Wander from gallery to gallery just watching the artists at work. There's plenty on sale, but standards are variable, so bargain hard.

North of Taman Sari, off Jalan Ngasem. Admission free.

Pasar Ngasem (Bird Market)

In this lively little market birds literally go for a song. Homing pigeons are snapped up for as little as Rp3,000; prize-winning turtle doves for more than Rp300,000. Occasionally you may come across yellow-crested parrots, fighting cocks or even baby Komodo dragons which are kept in buckets and used as a backdrop for less-than-exotic photographs.

Jalan Ngasem, north of Taman Sari. Admission free.

Sono Budoyo Museum, see Yogyacarta walk, pages 64–5.

Taman Sari (Fragrant Garden)

This famous little water palace, totally dedicated to pleasure with its sunken baths and underwater tunnels, was where the Sultan Hamengkubuwono I, his family and harem could escape from the cares of the world. Designed by a Portuguese architect and built in 1758, its idyllic existence was to prove short-lived, however, and following the sultan's death it was abandoned and subsequently destroyed by an earthquake. Guided tours take in the ruined gardens and underwater mosque,

---

WATER PALACES

Between 1765 and 1946, when king Gusti Bagus constructed the last of them, Balinese and Javanese kings and sultans were responsible for an abundance of water palaces and pleasure parks. Some had domes, others follies and pagoda-like thrones for the gods. So well planned was the Taman Sari in Yogyakarta, that it even provided water baths for the royal concubines.

ASPIRING ARTISANS
Impressed by the beautiful cloth painted with wax and dyed in dazzling colours known as batik? Most tourists are content merely to buy an example or two, but those who are sufficiently intrigued can attend day or week courses in the craft which are now advertised in several shops. There is even a Batik Research Centre on Jalan Sultan Agung.

but these days there is little else left of those happier times.
Jalan Taman, a 10-minute walk south of the Kraton. Open: daily, 9am–3pm. Admission charge.

Excursions
For a delightful tour of Yogya's neighbouring handicraft villages, either rent a taxi from outside your hotel, or better still hire an *Andong* (horse-drawn cart). First stop should be Kasongan (7km south), which is best known for its pottery and its copies of Javanese wooden dolls. Afterwards visit Kota Gede (6km southeast) with its fine silver jewellery. Finally, drop by the small village of Krantil, home to Pak Warno Waskito, one of the most famous living mask-makers of Yogya.

The famous Taman Sari was a favourite retreat of the sultan and his harem

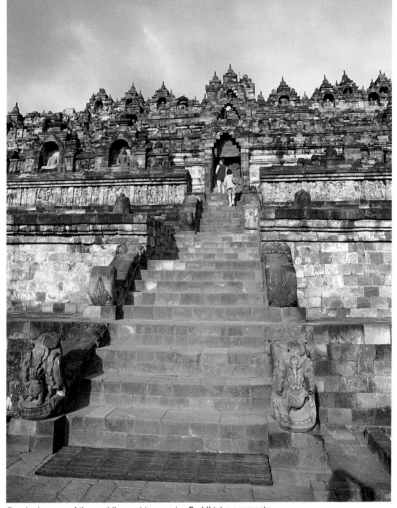

Borobudur, one of the world's most impressive Buddhist monuments

BOROBUDUR

One of the great wonders of the ancient world, the magnificent Borobudur complex lies just a short distance from Yogyakarta, rising up from the fertile Kudu Plain. You can see it from below, a doughnut-shaped structure made up of intricate reliefs, spired domes and serene Buddha images.

Built during the reign of the Sailendra dynasty between AD778 and 856,

Borobudur predates even the great Angkor Wat in Cambodia by nearly 300 years. Little is known of its early history, however, and shortly after its completion, Mount Merapi, the neighbouring volcano, erupted and Borobudur along with much of Central Java was mysteriously abandoned.

It was only in 1814 that the British Lieutenant-Governor of Java, Sir Thomas Stamford Raffles, was informed of the existence of the ruined temple and dispatched 200 men to uncover what was left. In 1907 restoration work got under way, but it took two world wars and another 76 years before the task was finally completed at a cost of US$25 million.

Location: 42km northwest of Yogyakarta. Buses run from the Umbulharjo terminal on Jalan Kemerdekan to Muntilan, from where you must catch another bus to the village of Borobudur. Most visitors simply take a tour. Open: daily, 6am–5pm. Admission charge.

Stone reliefs at Borobudur depict scenes from the life of the Buddha

Touring the Site

Most tours begin at the east gate, gradually working their way around the panels in an anti-clockwise fashion just as the many pilgrims did 10 centuries ago. By keeping the panels on your right, the journey will take you through 5km of corridors, past 72 *stupas* weighing as much as 600kg and containing more than 500 stone Buddhas.

Each level marks a gradual transition from *khamadhatu*, the world of desires, to *rupadhatu*, the sphere of form, and *arupadhatu* or *nirvana*, the ultimate perfection. Each terrace offers a different and richer perspective and the *mandala* shape of the monument is believed to symbolise the wheel of life and the infinite cycle of birth, death and rebirth.

As you reach the highest level, marked by circular terraces, you enter an area of formlessness with only a few *stupas* and dramatic views of distant mountains, a fitting end to the journey into the realms of perfection.

Etchings of Perfection

There is no need to look at all 1,400 relief panels as even a cursory glance at the 8,000 sq m of sculpting will provide rewards. The first series around the base depicts the transitory pleasures of worldly existence. Later panels show the birth of the Buddha and his journey from the confines of the palace to the valleys of the Ganges and his final enlightenment and release from suffering. You will find plenty of other reliefs, too, from the former lives of the Buddha as depicted in the Jataka Tales to depictions of the Buddhist cosmos, all executed with delicate and beautifully intricate detail.

The best time to view the reliefs is at dawn or dusk during the week. Wise people stay the night in the beautiful Borobudur Guesthouse; others in cheaper accommodation in the vicinity. Avoid weekends when the place is over-run.

Other Temples

If you have seen Borobudur and have the time, drop by the nearby temple complexes of Candi Mendut and Candi Pawon. While they cannot compare in scale, they do offer elaborate carvings from the Jataka Tales as well as a pleasant respite from the crowds.
3km east of Borobudur. Open: daily, 6am–5pm. Admission charge.

Sulphur springs at sunset on Dieng Plateau

DIENG PLATEAU

A stunning stretch of road that passes
steep gorges and mountains will bring
you to another of Central Java's great
hideaways, Dieng Plateau. Known as the
'abode of the gods', it is cooler than the
plains and commands a magnificent
setting amid sulphur springs, volcanic
lakes and ruined temples. Don't expect
up-market accommodation, though, or
many tour groups for that matter.
*Location: 117km northwest of Yogyakarta.
Buses run from Yogya's Umbulharjo
Terminal on Jalan Kemerdekan to
Magelang, from where you must catch
another bus to Wonoboso (25km) and then
a minibus to Dieng.*

Temples

To appreciate Dieng's temples at their
finest, view them at dawn when the
simple ruins are still shrouded in early-
morning mist. In all there are more than
100 of them, built between the 7th and
9th centuries by the Sailendra dynasty
and scattered over the northern part of
the valley. Eight temples have since been
restored. They are named after the
famed characters of the *Mahabarata* epic:
Arjuna, Srikandi, Semar, Puntadewa,
Sembadro and Gatot. All of them are
dedicated to Shiva.
*The entrance to the central plateau is a short
distance east of Dieng village. Admission
charge.*

Other Excursions
From the guesthouses in Dieng, guides
will take you to the Telega Warna
coloured lake (2km) and the awesome
Sikidang Crater (3km), as well as to a
nearby mountain-top from where to view
sunrise. Alternatively, get a map and just
wander among the sloping fields where
the locals cultivate cabbages and potatoes
against a backdrop of ruined temples.

GUNUNG MERAPI (Mount Merapi)
On a clear day, Mount Merapi can be
seen in all its glory and there are
magnificent views over the surrounding
region. But this 2,950m-high mountain is
also one of the world's most destructive
volcanoes, with six observation posts now
monitoring its activity 24 hours a day.
Enthusiastic climbers scale the mountain
in 6 hours; less fit mortals take
considerably longer. The best approach is
from the village of Selo, which can be
reached from Muntilan; and a guide is
strongly recommended. (See Getting
Away From it All, pages 134–5.)

KALIURANG
This delightful mountain resort on the
slopes of Mount Merapi is just a 1-hour

Join the locals on a horse-and-cart tour of
Parangtritis's beaches

ride from Yogyakarta, yet it offers
spectacular panoramas, fine walks and
cool mountain air as well as several
enchanting waterfalls. Stay away at
weekends.
Location: 24km north of Yogyakarta.
Regular buses leave from the main
Umbulharjo terminal on Jalan Kemerdekan,
taking 1 hour.

PARANGTRITIS
For a glimpse of blue ocean and crashing
waves, take this route south past rice
fields and banana plantations to the
beach resort of Parangtritis nestling
among spectacular cliffs and fringed by
sand dunes. Apart from taking a ride in a
horse-drawn cart, nibbling on fried squid
in one of the handful of drink stalls, or
taking long walks along the beach, there
isn't a lot to do here. You can paddle in
the sea, but don't swim in the vicious
undercurrents that take their toll every
year.
Location: 28km south of Yogyakarta.
Regular buses run from Umbulharjo
terminal on Jalan Kemerdekan, taking 50
minutes.

ENIGMATIC GODDESS
It is unwise to wear green in the
vicinity of Parangtritis's beach, or
indeed at Pangandaran or any of the
other neighbouring coastal areas, for
legend has it that this is the favourite
colour of the beloved Kangjeng Ratu
Kidul, Queen of the Southern Seas.
Swimmers who defy the warnings
risk being taken to the beautiful
goddess's underwater palace – on a
one-way ticket.

More than 220 temples make up the Prambanan complex

PRAMBANAN

Experts may consider Borobudur larger and more beautiful than Prambanan, but locals claim these imposing Hindu temples are among the finest in Asia. Built between the 9th and 10th centuries, and covering a vast area of undulating plains and rice fields, the great monuments were abandoned when the Sanjaya dynasty mysteriously moved to Eastern Java.

Following a great earthquake in the middle of the 16th century many of the temples fell into rack and ruin. Only over the last 40 years has extensive restoration taken place, with the main complex of temples being restored to its former glory.

Location: 17km northeast of Yogyakarta. Regular buses run from the Umbulharjo Terminal on Jalan Kemerdekan to Prambanan town, taking 45 minutes. From the bus stop, it is a short walk to the entrance to the historical park. Open: daily, 6am–6pm. Admission charge.

The Shiva Complex

The centrepiece of the Prambanan complex is not just another temple, but a veritable work of art carved with stone monkeys and heavenly parrots that soars 47m high. It is dedicated to Shiva the Destroyer.

To appreciate the full sequence of narrative reliefs, start to the left of the eastern stairway and proceed clockwise. Each of the panels shows a scene from the Hindu epic, the *Ramayana*, beginning at the palace of Rama's father and recounting the story of Rama's marriage to Sita, her kidnapping by the Demon King of Lanka and rescue by Hanuman, King of the monkeys.

Nor are bas-reliefs the only attraction. If you continue to the main eastern chamber you will find a 3m-tall, four-armed statue of Shiva standing on a huge lotus pedestal, covered in flowers left by devotees. Adjacent rooms contain other surprises, with the statues of the sage Agastya, his son Ganesh and Loro

Jonggrang, a formidable young virgin who was turned into stone for refusing to marry a love-struck giant.

Flanking the Shiva temple are two smaller temples dedicated to Vishnu the Protector and Brahma the Creator. Although these cannot compare in stature, they also contain fine reliefs from the _Ramayana_ and the _Mahabharata_, as well as carvings of heavenly nymphs trying to seduce the gods.

Further around the complex you can take your pick of another 224 smaller shrines, some of them renovated, others just piles of stone and broken memories. While most coach tours arrive in the late morning or afternoon, the best times to visit Prambanan are dawn and dusk when the temples are bathed in golden rays and infused with the silent power of times gone by: real enthusiasts should spend the night in one of the small guesthouses outside the park and experience both.

Candi Plaosan, Prambanan

Around Prambanan

Within a short distance of the main Prambanan complex are countless other temples, some of them undergoing restoration, others still in ruins. Candi Sewu, Candi Plaosan, Candi Kalasan and Candi Sari are all worth a visit. Ask a local guide to take you there, or better still take a bicycle or motorbike (see Prambanan drive, pages 66–7).

Ramayana Performances

Visitors in the vicinity of Prambanan between May and October on the nights of the full moon should not miss the performance of the _Ramayana_. This spectacle, set against the background of Candi Prambanan, brings together one of the leading dance groups on Java and provides one of the island's most memorable experiences. For information, call (0274) 96404 or ask at a travel agent in Yogyakarta.

SURAKARTA (SOLO)

Lovers of this bustling city of half a million inhabitants claim that Surakarta's charms are not only greater than those of neighbouring Yogyakarta, but that its attractions, which range from art galleries to the Sultan's Palace, are equally invigorating.

Known more often as Solo, this royal city also claims its place in history. During the 17th century the district was the seat of the Mataram Kingdom, the last of the great kingdoms in Central Java. Only in 1755 was the kingdom divided by the Dutch and a rival court established in neighbouring Yogyakarta.

These days there's still a Kraton to remind you of the grand old days, as well as wide, tree-lined streets, lively little markets and an air of relative calm.

Most visitors explore the town in a day, but Solo also makes a good base from which to explore the surrounding region with its hills and lush mountain resorts.

Location: 65km northeast of Yogyakarta. Buses leave from Yogya's Umbulharjo Terminal on Jalan Kemerdekan to Solo, taking 90 minutes. Trains run from the station on Jalan Pasar Kembang. Garuda and Sempati have direct flights to Adisumarmo Airport, 10km from Solo.

Kraton Surakarta

Legend has it that this palace, known as the Susuhunan's Palace, which means 'royal foot placed on the head of vassals paying homage', burnt down in January 1985 because its sultan did not pay sufficient attention to the powerful spirits. To make amends, the head of a tiger, a buffalo and a snake were offered up to the offended spirits, along with 30 truckloads of ashes, by throwing them into the sea at Parangtritis. The offerings appear to have done the trick and since then the newly rebuilt palace, along with its museum and richly gilded audience hall, have continued to thrive – as have the fortunes of Pagkubuwono XII, the sultan who occupies it.

Alun-Alun Square, south of Jalan Slamet Riyadi. Open: Monday to Thursday and Saturday, 8am–2pm; Sunday, 8am–3pm; closed Friday. Note that visitors are requested to wear a gold and red tassel as a mark of respect. Admission charge.

Mesjid Besar, see Surakarta walk, pages 68–9.

PURA MANGKUNEGARAN (Mangkunegaran Palace)

This 200-year-old palace, which was built for a junior line of the ruling house of Surakarta, contains a vast and

Pagkubuwono X (1893–1939) was responsible for the main decoration of Kraton Surakarta

Surakarta's sultans are still revered despite their fall from power

find the Museum Radya Pustaka which has a collection of *gamelan* instruments and shadow puppets.
Jalan Slamet Riyadi, to the west of the Kraton. Open: daily, 8am–10pm. Admission charge.

Excursions Around Solo
For delightful scenery with fine walks and waterfalls, leave Solo and catch a bus to the hill resort of Sarangan (53km) or the busier Tawangmangu (40km), situated on the slopes of Mount Lawu. Keen archaeologists can also explore the 15th-century Candi Sukuh (36km) with its ancient phallic objects hewn into the rock. For details of Sarangan and Tawangmangu see Getting Away From it All, pages 142–3.

intricately decorated pavilion, a shady garden divided in two – one side for women, the other for men – and a museum filled with ancient coins, masks, jewellery and even a chastity belt for the queen. On Saturday mornings, at 10am, you may be serenaded by musicians playing the palace's 200-year-old *gamelan*, known as 'the drifting of smiles'.
At the end of Jalan Diponegoro. Open: Monday to Saturday, 8am–2pm; Sunday, 8am–1pm. Admission charge includes guided tour.

Pasar Klewar, see Surakarta walk, pages 58–9.

THR Sriwedari Amusement Park
The perfect spot for relaxation. Visit a selection of animals from Central Java, nibble on sticks of pork *satay* under shady trees – and enjoy carnival rides and a children's playground. Next door you can

Some large sections of Kraton Surakarta escaped the fire of 1985

Yogyakarta

Starting out at the busy central market, this walk will take you past the old Dutch fort and presidential palace to the royal mosque and the Sultan's Palace. Afterwards, you can explore the colourful bird market. *Allow 3 hours.*

Begin at the central market known as Pasar Beringharjo on Jalan Jen A Yani.

1 PASAR BERINGHARJO

This is not only the biggest covered market in Yogyakarta, but by far the most intriguing with its dimly lit stalls selling every kind of tropical fruit as well as beautiful fabrics, baskets and motorbike spare parts. Beware of pick-pockets though, and persuasive touts who will take a commission on whatever you buy.

Walk south down Jalan Jen A Yani for 250m and on your left you will find the Benteng Budaya.

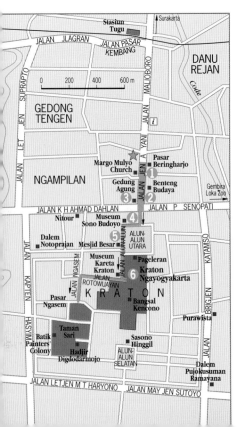

2 BENTENG BUDAYA

Locals call this fine old building Fort Vredeburgh, after the Dutch garrison which was built here in 1765 to house 500 troops; it also served as the local gaol. The government has since turned the place into a museum containing exhibits of Yogyakarta's history, featuring especially its exploits in the war for independence.

Leave the museum and almost directly opposite you will see the Gedung Agung.

3 GEDUNG AGUNG (STATE GUESTHOUSE)

This elegant building set amid lush gardens and fruit trees was built in 1823 as the Dutch president's mansion and rebuilt in 1869 following an earthquake. Between 1946 and 1949, when Yogyakarta was declared capital of the founding republic, it served as the presidential palace. Today it is closed to the public.

Continue straight over the main road (Jalan P Senopati) to Alun-Alun Utara and on your right you will see the Museum Sono Budoyo.

4 MUSEUM SONO BUDOYO (NATIONAL ART MUSEUM)

You will find some of the best Javanese, Balinese and Madurese art in this fine little museum as well as stone carvings and the shadow puppets known as Wayang Kulit. Keep an eye open for the famous statue of the monkey god Hanuman, and a bridal suite dedicated to the goddess of rice and fertility.

Leave the museum and continue along Jalan Alun-Alun until you see the Mesjid Besar a short distance ahead on your right.

5 MESJID BESAR (GRAND MOSQUE)

Despite its rather ordinary appearance the royal mosque, which was built in 1773 under Sultan Harmengubuwono I, has an unusual triple-layered roof as well as some striking engraved gold doors. Every September, during the colourful Gunungan procession, hundreds of believers walk to the mosque carrying mounds of rice, peanuts and chillies which they leave as offerings.

Continue south along Jalan Alun-Alun until you reach the entrance to the Kraton on your left.

6 KRATON

This building is the veritable seat of power in Yogyakarta and is inhabited by the revered Sultan Hamengkubuwono X. It was built in 1755 during the reign of Hamengkubuwono I and is largely symbolic of Mount Meru, centre of the

A retainer of the sultan, Kraton Yogyakarta

cosmos. A short distance behind the Kraton, on Jalan Rotowijayan, you will find the ancient royal stables.

From the Kraton walk down Jalan Rotowijayan and turn left at the intersection with Jalan Ngasem. At the end of the road either catch a tricycle back to your hotel or continue to the Pasar Ngasem Bird Market (see pages 54–5).

OPENING DETAILS

Benteng Budaya. Open: Tuesday to Thursday and Sunday, 8am– 4pm; Friday, 8am–11am; Saturday, 8am–1pm.

Museum Sono Budoyo. Open: Tuesday to Thursday and Sunday, 8am– 4pm; Friday, 8am–11am; Saturday, 8am–1pm.

Kraton. Open: Saturday to Thursday, 8am–2pm; Friday, 9am–11am. Stables are open daily, 8am–4pm. Admission charge.

Prambanan

Starting from the recently discovered Candi Sambisari, this tour will take you to the magnificent Candi Prambanan as well as to several smaller and lesser-known temples near by. You will need to arrange transport before you go. *Allow a full day.*

Take the main road east from Yogyakarta towards Prambanan and at the 12.5km marker turn left and drive 2km north to Candi Sambisari.

1 CANDI SAMBISARI

Although this small *candi* was only discovered in 1966 by a local farmer, it has since been excavated along with three smaller temples dedicated to Shiva. Inside are several fine carvings of Ganesh as well as some unfinished reliefs which may have been abandoned following a sudden volcanic eruption.

From Candi Sambisari, return to the main road and continue for 3km until you see a signpost for Candi Kalasan on the right.

2 CANDI KALASAN

One of the oldest Buddhist shrines in the area, Candi Kalasan may date back as far as AD778, although restoration has since taken place. Next to the southern doorway you will see beautifully decorated stone reliefs. The temple also contains one large and three small chambers inhabited by great numbers of bats.

Continue along the road towards Prambanan and after 200m turn

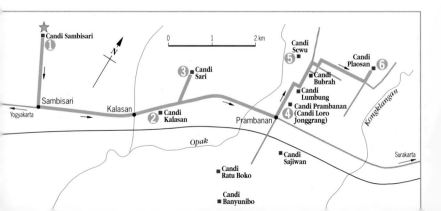

left to Candi Sari, signposted a short distance off the main road.

3 CANDI SARI

Set in delightful scenery of banana and coconut groves, this square temple was once a Buddhist sanctuary and contains 36 panels of dancing goddesses, musicians and Buddhist deities. It was built some time during the 9th century, although extensively restored in 1929. Around the windows you will find small niches overlooked by stern *kala* heads.

From Candi Sari return to the main road, turn left and head towards Prambanan village. Turn left at the crossroads for Candi Prambanan.

4 CANDI PRAMBANAN

This magnificent complex is one of the finest single monuments in all Indonesia and is the biggest and best-known Hindu *candi* in the country. It was completed during the 10th century to commemorate the victory of the Sanjaya dynasty over the Buddhist Sailendra kings of Central Java, but was deserted a few years later. Explore the great Shiva temple, which is 47m tall, and the two smaller shrines dedicated to Vishnu and Brahma.

From Prambanan Temple follow the signpost for Candi Sewu, which lies 1.5km to the north.

5 CANDI SEWU

This complex, known as the 'thousand temples', contains just 240 shrines and was built around AD850. Renovation was completed in 1993 and you can now admire finely carved galleries, the main temple and the two large statues brandishing clubs which guard the entrance from evil spirits.

From Candi Sewu drive 1.5km to the east

The carved reliefs of celestrial beings on Candi Sari were originally painted in bright colours

along the main road and you will find Candi Plaosan on your left.

6 CANDI PLAOSAN

This delightful complex consists of a large rectangular temple surrounded by a number of shrines and *stupas* believed to date from the 9th century. Inside the main temple you will find six beautiful stone statues of Buddha along with reliefs of worshippers. A short walk south will bring you to the Plaosan Kidul, made up of a ruined complex currently undergoing extensive restoration work.

From Candi Plaosan either continue to the small temples of Candi Sajiwan and Candi Ratu Boko, which lie further south, or head back to Yogyakarta.

Surakarta (Solo)

Jakarta

JAVA
Yogyakarta • Surakarta • Surabaya

Starting at the Kraton Surakarta, this walk will take you from ancient pavilions and audience halls to the local batik market and the royal mosque. From here it is a pleasant stroll to the city's other famous landmark, the Mangkunegaran Palace. *Allow 3 hours.*

Begin at the Kraton Surakarta Hadingrat, situated off Jalan Kratonan in the south of town.

1 KRATON SURAKARTA HADINGRAT

The centrepiece of Solo was built in 1745 by King Pakubuwana II and contains several pavilions and an elegant marble

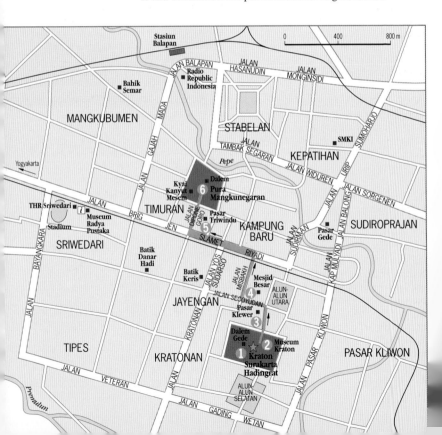

audience hall. Although much of the Kraton was burnt down in January 1985, Susuhunan's private residence and meditation chamber have since been restored.

Next door to the Kraton you will find the Museum Kraton.

2 MUSEUM KRATON

Housed in this museum built around a courtyard you will find a collection of 200 to 300-year-old royal carriages as well as fine bronze statues, ceremonial outfits and demonic figureheads. If you want to take photographs, remember to obtain a special ticket at the entrance.

Leave the museum and on your left, on Jalan Secoyudan, you will find Pasar Klewer.

3 PASAR KLEWER

Inside this two-storey concrete block is one of the largest batik markets in Indonesia. You can buy anything from best silk to flamboyant western boxer shorts. Remember to bargain.

Leave Pasar Klewer and almost directly opposite, on Jalan Secoyudan, you will see the Mesjid Besar.

4 MESJID BESAR (GRAND MOSQUE)

The most impressive aspect of this incongruous looking mosque is its sheer size. Pakubuwana III built the original structure in 1750 although it has since been enlarged by various Sultans to occupy an area of 3.5 hectares. There are plenty of other points of interest too, from its Middle Eastern-style minaret to its Javanese-style traditional peaked roofs. Visitors are welcome, but dress neatly and wash your hands and feet before entering the mosque.

Exit the mosque and follow the road around until you reach Jalan Brig Jen Slamet Riyadi. Turn left and 800m further on turn right on to Jalan Diponegoro. You will find Pasar Triwindu on your right.

5 PASAR TRIWINDU (ANTIQUE MARKET)

This delightful little flea market offers almost everything you can dream of from ancient paintings and masks to puppets and an abundance of fake antiques and curios.

Leave Pasar Triwindu and continue along Jalan Diponegoro. At the end of the road you will see the Pura Mangkunegaran.

6 PURA MANGKUNEGARAN

Although smaller and less well known than the Kraton Surakarta, this palace built by a branch of the Surakarta royal family has beautiful gardens, birds and European-style fountains as well as a vast audience pavilion which was until recently the largest on Java. The palace was begun by Mangkunegoro I at the end of the 18th century and completed in 1866. Behind the audience pavilion is the museum with a collection of antique jewellery, coins and chastity belts.

Leave the palace and walk to the main road, Jalan Brig Jen Slamet Riyadi, from where you will be able to catch a tricycle back to your hotel.

OPENING DETAILS
Kraton Surakarta Hadingrat. See page 62 for opening times.
Museum Kraton. See Kraton opening times. Admission included in price of entry to Kraton..
Pura Mangkunegaran. Open: Monday to Saturday, 8am–2pm; Sunday, 8am–1pm.

East Java

*E*ast Java, stretching narrowly down from Ngawi to the port of Ketapang, is the least visited part of Java, offering national parks and volcanoes along with hill resorts and a staggering lunar landscape. If you are travelling overland to Bali, it's easy to visit Mount Bromo or the lesser-known Baluran National Park. Buses travel between all the major towns, and trains connect Surabaya with Jakarta, Surakarta, Probolinggo and Banyuwangi. For an easy hop, you can take the plane to Surabaya from Jakarta or Denpasar on Bali.

SURABAYA

Most visitors tend to miss out Surabaya, the big busy industrial town which lies a short distance from the coast, but the provincial capital of East Java does offer reasonable hotels and a tourist office, as well as some of the friendliest inhabitants in the whole of Java. It is also a good stopping point before visiting Mount Bromo or the nearby island of Madura.

During the struggle for Indonesia's independence, Surabaya was a major centre of resistance against the Dutch. At one stage, in 1945, it was even bombed by the British who led an assault on the city in which thousands of Indonesians were killed. Today, the heroes' monument, situated in the centre of town, stands as a proud reminder of Surabaya's contribution to the nation's founding.

Location: 780km east of Jakarta. Buses leave for all the major towns and cities from the main bus terminal on the corner of Jalan Yani and Jalan Sutoyo. Trains take 15 hours to Jakarta and 4.5 hours to Surakarta. There are also flights to Bali, Lombok and major destinations on Java from Juanda Airport, 18km to the south of town.

Jembatan Merah (Red Bridge)

For a glimpse of the old Dutch commercial district with its run-down warehouses and turn-of-the-century office buildings, visit

Monument recalling Surabaya's role in the struggle for independence

The charming but dilapidated backstreets around Jembatan Merah, Surabaya

the area around this famous bridge which was the scene of heavy fighting during the battle for Surabaya in 1945. Hire a tricyclist to take you to such famous buildings as Grahadi, the former residence of the Dutch governor, as well as the Majapahit Hotel – or just explore the labyrinth of little alleyways to the west of the bridge.

Jalan Rajawali, in the northern part of town, a short distance from Tugu Pahlawan.

Kebun Binatang (Surabaya Zoo)
More than 500 species of animals and exotic birds are crammed into the Surabaya Zoo along with flying squirrels, dolphins, dwarf buffalo and the biggest attraction of all, a Komodo dragon. Don't expect to see the animals accommodated with many comforts though. The cages are small and the place crowded for much of the time.

Jalan Raya Diponegoro, in the south of town. Open: daily, 7am–6pm. Admission charge.

Pasar Sore
Between 6pm and 9pm this little street is a solid row of stalls selling anything from T-shirts to antique alarm clocks .

Jalan Pandegiling.

Tanyung Perak Harbour
Although not officially a tourist spot, the harbour does play host to several delightful wooden Schooners. Frequent boats also leave from the adjacent quay to the island of Madura at regular intervals, 24 hours a day.

Jalan Kalimas Baru, in the north of the city. Ask the taxi driver to take you to Pelabuhan Tanyung Perak.

Tugu Pahlawan (Heroes' Monument)
This rather uninspiring monument in the centre of the main square was built to commemorate the valiant struggle of the Surabaya people against the Dutch, and especially for the thousands who died when British troops attacked the city on 10 November 1945.

Jalan Pahlawan.

Crossing the sand sea at spectacular Mount Bromo

BALURAN TAMAN NASIONAL (Baluran National Park)

You can't go further east than Baluran National Park, unless you cross over into Bali, but this 240 sq km game reserve set amid arid savannah and surrounded on three sides by the sea has no shortage of attractions. If you visit the park between the months of June and November, when wildlife is more plentiful, you may well catch rare glimpses of wild pigs and barking deer, as well as countless birds, monkeys and huge wild oxen. Make sure that you contact the PHPA office at the park entrance to obtain a permit and organise accommodation, and take food if you intend to stay overnight. Guides are available to take you on walks.
Location: 280km east of Surabaya (tel: Banyuwangi 41118). Buses run from Surabaya and from Ketapang (37km), the arrival and departure point for ferries to Bali. Ask to be dropped off at the park headquarters. Admission charge.

BATU/SELEKTA

These neighbouring towns with their fine views of Mount Arjuna make popular weekend retreats from the plains below. Batu is larger and more suburban, but with fine walks and lively markets. Selekta is more up-market, with bubbling streams, orchards and pine trees.
Location: 23km northwest of Malang. Irregular buses leave from Malang's Dinoyo station on Jalan Haryono. Alternatively, agree a price and take a taxi.

GUNUNG BROMO (Mount Bromo)

The jewel in the crown of East Java's tourist industry lies about an hour's drive from Probolinggo, high up in the Tengger mountains, surrounded by volcanic peaks and craters. Mount Bromo offers awesome views and a desolate landscape that is not easy to find elsewhere in Indonesia.

As you take the spectacular road up to Cemara Lawang you will see

TEMPESTUOUS LOVE
Were it not for a love-struck ogre and a beautiful princess, Bromo might have looked like any other volcano. But when, according to legend, the unsightly lover was rejected he flung a half coconut shell on to the ground – which turned into Mount Batok – then leapt into the fiery crater.

Tenggerese guides

magnificent vistas of rice fields and cabbage fields clutching on to almost sheer mountainsides, every little area cultivated. Some visitors come here for the journey alone, but the majority arrive at dawn to watch the sun come up over the vast sea of sand and all the big hotels and package tours now run these early-morning trips from Surabaya. A cheaper and more adventurous way though is to take a *bemo* from the nearby town of Probolinggo (40km) and spend the night in one of the small hotels or guesthouses in Cemara Lawang. Remember to take warm clothes and a torch.
Location: 3-hour drive southeast of Surabaya. Buses run from Surabaya to the town of Probolinggo. From here you must take a crowded minibus to Ngadisari (40km) and then another minibus 3km further to Cemara Lawang, the departure point for Bromo. Alternatively, for a touch of comfort, simply charter a minibus from Probolinggo.

Climbing the Summit
You won't need a guide to take you up to the summit. These days literally hundreds of tourists make the pre-dawn trek, and locals are on hand with horses to carry you to the foot of the mountain. Allow an hour if you are walking from the village of Cemara Lawang. As you cross the sand

sea and begin climbing the 250 steps that lead up the rim of the volcano you will be able to smell the sulphur like some malodorous form of methane gas. Bromo, however, though live, has not erupted for many years and is considered to be one of the safest volcanoes on Java. After watching the dawn come up, some people then walk the entire way round the vast crater. Be warned, however; the rim is extremely narrow in some parts and accidents are by no means unheard of.

Exploring the Area
The majority of visitors simply bus into Bromo from Probolinggo, watch the sunrise and bus out again. A better alternative is to spend the day exploring the area. Visit Mount Penanggungan (6km away) with its magnificent views of Bromo and Gunung Semeru, one of the most active volcanoes in the whole of Indonesia. To arrange a jeep, visitors staying at the Cemara Indah Hotel can simply contact the manager. Failing that, negotiate a price with any of the *bemo* drivers in the village. It is also possible to trek from Cemara Lawang to Ngadas (8km) on the southern rim of the Tengger crater, although you should allow a full day and seek information locally.

Distant Gunung Semeru viewed from Mount Penanggungan

GUNUNG SEMERU (Mount Semeru)

One of the most beautiful and highest peaks on Java, this mountain, known as Mehameru (great mountain), reaches 3,600m. You can climb it in two days with camping equipment and a guide but make sure you enquire about conditions locally since volcanic eruptions have become something of a Semeru speciality.

Location: access is from the small village of Rano Pani, to the east of Malang. Buses run via Tumpang, Gubug Klakah and Ngadas. Accommodation consists of one rest house.

MADURA ISLAND

Legend has it that the best lovers in the whole of Indonesia come from the poor and arid island of Madura, along with the swiftest running bulls. To see them both, visit the island between August and October when the famous races are held in several of the major towns and villages. Make sure that you get the precise dates from the regional tourist office in Surabaya (tel: 575 448) as the timing of the event changes from year to year.

Location: 1-hour boat trip from Surabaya. Boats leave regularly 24 hours a day from Tanyung Perak Harbour on Jalan Kalimas Baru to Kamal, on the southwest coast of Madura. Jeeps circulate the island at regular intervals, but tourist services are almost non-existent.

MALANG

Situated on the banks of the Sungai Brantas River, the busy town of Malang boasts numerous parks, tree-lined streets and villas. Only 150 years ago, the Dutch turned it into a centre for the production of coffee and tobacco, and these days they return in vast numbers to admire its colonial architecture and spotlessly clean streets. For something special, visit the famous Candi Singosari (10km north), built by the Singosari dynasty at the turn of the 13th century, or the 13th-century Candi Jawi (49km north).

Location: 90km south of Surabaya. Buses to Surabaya, Probolinggo and Jakarta leave from the Arjosari terminal on Jalan Intan. Trains for Surabaya and Jakarta depart from the station on Jalan Kerta Negara.

A diet of beer helps turn Madura's fleet-footed bulls into winners

BOISTEROUS BULLS

Beginning with the wave of a red flag and ending 9 seconds later with screams from the crowd, the famous bull races of Madura have become known as one of the major attractions of the island. Specially trained bulls dressed in fine colours parade before the crowds to the fortifying sounds of *gamelan* music. The winners of the 100m races bring fame not only to their owners, but to entire villages, while the top bulls merrily retire to father the next generation of champions.

Bali

*I*ndonesia's favourite tropical hideaway nestles just 2km from the eastern tip of Java, surrounded by lush paddies and shimmering white beaches. On Bali, the flowers appear to be always in bloom and every day is a celebration of the beneficence of the gods. Temples dot the towns and villages whilst thousands of spirit houses watch over the well-being of the island's 3 million inhabitants.

When the first European sailors came across this earthly paradise, they simply jumped ship and it took the captain more than two years to round them all back up. Later, artists settled in Ubud, enchanted by the people and their Hindu culture.

These days almost a million tourists arrive on Bali every year, swamping its beaches, piling into its temples and turning parts of the island into the Torremolinos of Asia.

Sun, sea and religion, Bali's recipe for success is epitomised at Candi Dasa

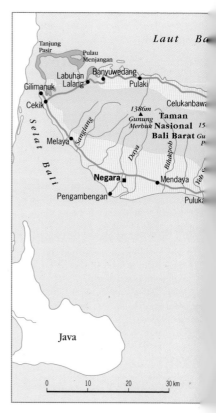

But although Kuta and some of the other popular tourist destinations have inevitably declined, it's easy to escape the crowds by going into the rice fields around Ubud or the unspoiled coastline of the east. From the peak of Mount Batur you can witness the magnificent sunrise over the lake and elsewhere view more than 20,000 temples built to honour the gods and lovingly tended by the Hindu people.

Nor should anyone miss the opportunity to attend a cremation or a temple festival.

Above all, however, it is the culture that most impresses visitors; the fleeting sense of spiritual calm and the Balinese religion which, despite the pervading air of commercialism, somehow continues to survive and thrive.

Although tours now operate excursions to almost every major site on the island, it is just as easy to arrange your own transport.

BALI

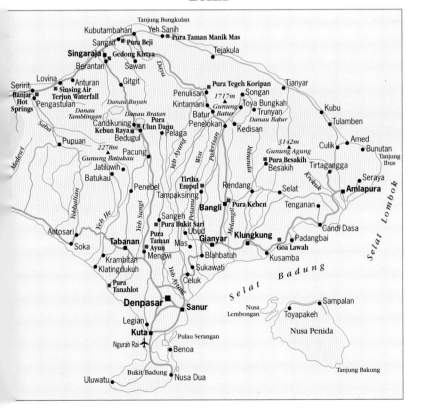

Coastal Bali

Almost everyone will, at some stage, visit Bali's tropical beaches. Most tourists opt for Kuta or the more up-market Sanur or Nusa Dua, but beyond these well-known resorts there are plenty of less highly developed areas, not necessarily as beautiful, but having the charm of relative isolation. Getting around from one resort to the other is easy. *Bemos* (minibuses) run regularly and for trips further afield buses, motorbikes, jeeps or (for the fit) bicycles are all good alternatives.

KUTA BEACH

Sun-tanned Australians don't travel to Kuta Beach without good reason, for this 10km stretch of sand has not only become the island's best-known surfers' paradise, but its most crowded and flamboyant Western playground.

From the moment you set foot in the place you will be sucked into a world that has no comparison. From the crowds of topless sunbathers to the surfers, masseurs and hustlers, Kuta literally seethes with life. Modern-day lotus-eaters can take their pick of a host of elderly masseurs who, for a price, will pummel every part of your anatomy with coconut oil. You can also get your hair plaited, buy a wooden 'antique' elephant and drink a Fosters beer – almost simultaneously.

Inland, beyond the beach, you'll find restaurants, markets selling hippie gear and literally hundreds of tour agencies, money-changers, motorbike rentals, *losmen* (guesthouses), and a growing number of classy hotels. And while the old hands may lament the demise of dreamy Kuta, there are plenty of newcomers who have no wish to go any further.

To find accommodation, simply wander along the *gangs* (alleyways) or take a taxi. There's something for just about every taste. Indeed, the only thing there isn't much of here is tranquillity, so if that is what you are after, try Sanur or Nusa Dua.

Location: 9km south of Denpasar. Taxis run from Ngurah Rai International Airport to Kuta Beach, taking 15 minutes. Regular bemos *ply the roads between Kuta and Tegal terminal in Denpasar. Buses to most tourist destinations can be booked through any travel agent.*

Watersports and Waves

For a touch of excitement, hire a surfboard and hit the water with a splash. Almost every shop rents them out by the day. The best surf is between March and July, but at virtually any time of the year you'll find ample-sized waves. Make sure, however, that you swim between the signposted water towers and red flags, which are patrolled by Australian-trained Balinese life savers, as dangerous rip-tides lead to regular drownings.

For gentler activity, experience a half-hour massage, a manicure or a hair plait. When you have had enough of the crowds and the hustlers peddling vulgar wooden carvings, you can wander north along the beach past Legian, the neighbouring village, and the Bali Oberoi as far as Seminyak for a touch of calm.

After Dark

At night, everything you could think of is

Choose your wave on Bali's best-known surfing beach, Kuta Beach

on offer in Kuta, from tranquil restaurants on lotus ponds to cafés and pizzerias. Pubs, discos and bars line the roads serving food and drink to the sound of a unique cocktail of heavy rock, reggae, or even *gamelan* music, and you can have a game of darts, enter a beer-drinking competition or simply attend one of the dance shows specially laid on for tourists in the big hotels.

Tours from Kuta

Kuta's band of tour agencies offers packages to suit every taste, from the shoestring to the luxurious. Popular sights in the vicinity include Uluwatu Temple (20km), Pantai Suluban (22km) and Tanahlot (40km).

One of the many luxury hotels that are the life and soul of Nusa Dua

NUSA DUA

Rising up from the Bukit Peninsula amid mangroves and dazzling tropical lawns, Nusa Dua (where the Reagans stayed) has become Bali's showcase resort, home not only to the most exclusive hotels on the island, but to its biggest convention centres. Here the roads are perfectly tarmacked and clipped hedges, fountains and beautiful sculptures abound.

Started in the mid-1970s with loans granted by the World Bank, this vast complex now comprises more than 3,000 luxury rooms with magnificent views and white sand, with the bonus of being able to stroll along the sea front without being hounded by vendors and masseurs. Enthusiastic sportsmen have a choice of tennis, health clubs, horse riding or an 18-hole international golf course. In addition, each hotel offers fine restaurants decked out with exotic tropical plants and palm trees where you can feast yourself on delicious, if expensive, seafood while watching a display of Balinese dancing.

Don't expect to get a feel for the real Bali here, however; the security guards who stop 'undesirable' local elements from entering the grounds also isolate you from a culture that predates the Hyatt and Sheraton Hotels by thousands of years. *Location: 25km south of Denpasar. Taxis take 20 minutes from Ngurah Rai International Airport, although many hotels*

lay on minibuses. Regular bemos *connect Nusa Dua with Denpasar's Tegal Terminal and with Kuta Beach.*

Benoa Village
Watersports lovers don't bother too much with Nusa Dua these days. After all, with Benoa village just a short distance to the north, there is little reason to. Here you'll find windsurfing, parasailing, scuba diving and jet skiing. Less energetic visitors can hire a boat to nearby Turtle Island (Pulau Serangan), or sit at expensive cafés on the beach feasting on fresh fish and prawns caught by local fishermen.
5km north of Nusa Dua. Most hotels run minibuses at any time of day.

SOUTHERN BALI

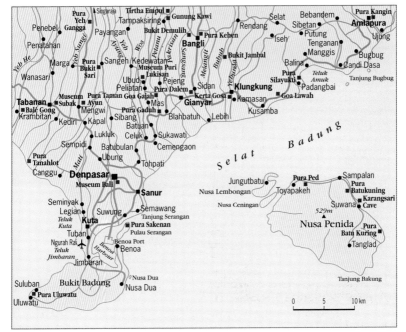

Enchanting paintings and sculpture at the Museum le Mayeur

The beach stretches for about 3km and there is a fine lagoon with a coral reef where, at dawn and dusk, you can see fishermen hard at work. Here, too, you can catch one of the colourful *prahu* fishing boats that ply the shores sailing to Turtle Island, or go further afield to the less visited islands of Nusa Lembongan and Nusa Penida. Note, however, that at low tide sea urchins can abound along Sanur Beach and swimming can be poor.

In the evening there is plenty of entertainment to be had, ranging from leafy restaurants to Balinese dances, and, for those of modern heart, discos. *Location: 7km east of Denpasar. Taxis run from Ngurah Rai International Airport, taking 15 minutes. Regular* bemos *operate between Sanur and Kreneng Terminal in Denpasar.*

Museum le Mayeur

This museum set in charming gardens contains some fine sculptures and paintings. The house was originally inhabited by Belgian artist Le Mayeur, who moved here in 1932 and resided in Sanur for more than 25 years. Le

SANUR

With one of the most beautiful stretches of beach on the island, plus a fleet of fishing boats and a touch of culture, Sanur offers something for everyone. You won't find many hippies here, either, or too much cheap accommodation, but you will find a scene that is considerably more relaxed than Kuta Beach and more natural than Nusa Dua.

During the 1930s the great Belgian artist Adrien Le Mayeur settled at Sanur, attracted by its pristine waters and exotic location. More recently the beach front has played host to growing numbers of hotel developments, but even these, with the exception of the Bali Beach and the Bali Hyatt, are bungalow-style with lush shady gardens and swimming pools.

A TOUCH OF HISTORY

Sanur may be better known for its beaches than its history, but in fact the village is not without the latter. In 1906 the Dutch fought a pitched battle along the sea front, then in 1943 it was the turn of the Japanese who landed here. In 1946 the Dutch retook Sanur, with the tranquil beaches only regaining their sparkle with independence some three years later.

Above: early morning on Sanur Beach
Right: fishermen take tours to Turtle Island

Mayeur died in 1958, a decade before the opening of the first big tourist hotel, but the house remains and is looked after by his widow Ni Polok, formerly one of Bali's greatest Legong dancers. Explore the interior with its works of art from Africa, Europe and the South Pacific, as well as Bali, and afterwards relax in the luxuriant little garden with its diminutive pond sporting goldfish.

Next to the Bali Beach Hotel. Open: Tuesday, Thursday and Sunday, 8am–2pm; Friday and Saturday, 8am–11am. Admission charge.

Pulau Serangan (Turtle Island)
Although the appealing sounding Turtle Island is promoted in Sanur as one of the great trips, most visitors find the place considerably overrated; it is full of crowds of tourists who stream over to buy expensive shells and to stare at miserable-looking green-back turtles in a muddy pond. Besides the highly revered temple of Pura Sakenan situated to the north of the island, the chief attraction is the beaches on the east coast. Even these are hard to get to though, and visitors constantly complain of the hassle and cost.

Public boats leave from Suwung, 1km south of Sanur. Boats can also be rented in Sanur or from Nusa Dua and Benoa. Day tours can be booked at any of the hotels.

Around the Coast

AMED

This little fishing village with its black sandy beaches and fine views of Mount Agung makes a perfect break either on the journey north or as part of a more extended island circuit. Currently there is no accommodation in Amed itself, but visitors wanting to stay the night will find cottages in neighbouring Bunutan (4km). As a pleasant side-trip, take the winding road along the coast to Ujung and Amlapura (see the Amlapura drive, pages 94–5).

Location: 22km north of Amlapura. Irregular bemos run via Culik, although private transport is recommended

Mount Agung viewed from Amed

BALI BARAT NATIONAL PARK, see
Getting Away From it All, page 141.

BALINA BEACH

Diving enthusiasts can explore some of the richest marine life on Bali from this little fishing village situated halfway up the eastern coast. Resorts organise diving trips to Nusa Penida, Nusa Lembongan and Pulau Menjangan and also rent out diving equipment. Although there is now plenty of accommodation, the feeling of relative isolation remains.

Location: 5km west of Candi Dasa. Bemos run from Klungkung and Candi Dasa. You will have to walk the short distance from the main road to the beach.

BENOA PORT

Cruise ships, yachts and oil tankers anchor at this harbour that juts out east of the airport. There's little other reason to come here, though, except to visit the Bali International Yacht Club.

Location: 9km south of Denpasar.

CANDI DASA

Visitors wanting to avoid the big, brassy beach resorts of the south coast thought they had discovered a pleasant alternative when they came across this sleepy little village. But in the years since it was established, Candi Dasa (pronounced Chandi Dasa) has rapidly joined the ranks of crowded resort areas and much of the beach has now been washed away along with the outlying reef. There are, however, plenty of bungalows squeezed into lush gardens with views of the breaking waves and the hills across the bay. You can take brightly coloured fishing boats to Nusa Penida, explore the beautiful lagoon at the eastern end of the beach and take your pick of countless bars and restaurants famed for their fresh fish and chocolate cake.

Location: 69km northeast of Denpasar. Bemos run from the Batubulan terminal, 6km to the northeast of town. Nearby destinations: Padangbai (15km), Tenganan Village (3km) and Balina (5km).

Candi Dasa's rapid ascent to resortdom has triggered the erosion of its beaches

GILIMANUK

Situated on the western tip of Bali, a 3–4-hour trip from Kuta, this busy little port links Bali with East Java and the town of Ketapang. Ferries run regularly, day and night, taking just 30 minutes to cross the narrow strait. It's a pleasant enough trip with few hassles and reasonable bus connections on either side.

Location: 128km northwest of Denpasar. Regular buses run from Denpasar's Ubung terminal on Jalan Cokroaminoto, taking 3 hours. Nearby attractions include the Bali Barat National Park, which lies 3km south (see Getting Away From it All, page 140).

GOA LAWAH

Thousands of squeaking bats pack the entrance to Goa Lawah Cave and temple. They hang upside-down and deposit large amounts of droppings on even larger amounts of visitors. Legend has it that the bats provide sustenance for the legendary giant snake, Naga Basuki, which resides somewhere in the gloomy depths beyond.

The cave can even boast a little history: earlier this century, in 1904, the kings of Bali held a conference here to plan an attack against the Dutch armies.

Location: 9km east of Klungkung on the route to Padangbai. Ask to be dropped off at the entrance. Admission to the temple is by donation.

Goa Lawah and its colony of bats

FISHERMEN

At dusk, as the first oil lamps begin to flicker in the small village of Kusamba which lies under the shadow of distant Mount Agung, the fishermen push out their colourful outriggers, known as *prahus*, on to the sand and from there into the sea. By the time darkness falls the bay is bespeckled with white sails hovering a few hundred metres from the shore, their nets submerged in the darkened swell.

These fishermen go out every night, regardless of whether the sea is stormy or calm, earning little more than Rp2,000 for their back-breaking labour. For up to 10 hours at a stretch they remain out in the bay, rocked by the ebbing of the tide as they cast their nets in the hope of a good catch.

Apart from calling on the goodwill of the deities, they also make offerings to Batter Braun, god of the sea, and paint the bows of their vessels with a large pair of eyes so that the boats can find their way.

The boats themselves consist of little more than a carved-out tree trunk propped up by large bamboo poles on either side. But the rickety appearance is misleading, for these boats not only catch barramundi and sea perch, but occasionally shark.

By dawn the first fishermen are back on shore, some of them carrying piles of freshly caught tuna, others with little to show for their efforts. A few women wait on the sand, ready to sell the morning's catch.

Left: fresh catch
Above: fishermen at dawn
Right: after the trawl

Salt farming provides an important source of income in the Kusamba area

KUSAMBA

It's just a short distance from the bat cave of Goa Lawah to the fishing village of Kusamba with its black sandy beaches, its colourful boats and straggling groups of salt-panners. Most people come here to take the uncomfortable 2- or 3-hour boat trip to the island of Nusa Penida, but a better alternative is to continue to neighbouring Padangbai (9km) where there is accommodation and a more regular service.

Location: 8km east of Klungkung. Regular bemos run on route for Padangbai and Amlapura. Nearby attractions include the Goa Lawah Bat Cave (3km).

LEBIH

The best time to visit this little coastal village is during one of the famed ritual purification ceremonies. At other times of the year there are only black-sand beaches and fishing boats, plus a few other tourists to share them with.

Location: 8km south of Gianyar. Catch an irregular bemo.

LOVINA BEACH

If you are looking for white sparkling beaches and tropical palms, then give Lovina a miss. Visitors who are happy with black sand and a relaxed atmosphere can, however, find plenty of consolation. Small bungalows and more up-market developments now line the coastline almost as far as Singaraja, and you can take your pick of the bunch. There are plenty of opportunities, too, for snorkelling, fishing or boat trips out to the nearby reef. Perhaps the highlight, though, is the dolphin tour at dawn when leaping fish can be seen silhouetted against the rising sun. Almost every guesthouse or hotel will either organise the trip or point you in the direction of someone who will. Day trips can easily be made to the Sinsing Air Terjun Waterfall (6km), the hot springs of Banjar (12km) or the beautiful Pura Beji temple beyond Singaraja (16 km).

Location: 10km west of Singaraja. Buses run from Denpasar's Ubung terminal, on Jalan Cokroaminoto, to Singaraja, from where there are regular bemos to Lovina and the neighbouring villages.

NUSA PENIDA AND NUSA LEMBONGAN

Years ago, the island of Nusa Penida was a penitentiary for criminals and other undesirable subjects. These days, visitors wanting to get away from it all have taken a liking to the place, although much of the island is poor and arid and the place renowned for the power of its demons. Several sites are worth visiting though. Stop by the Pura Ped temple complex (4km east of Toyapakeh) to see the dwelling place of the evil monster Ratu Gede Macaling, or visit the Karangsari limestone cave 6km south of Sampalan.

From Nusa Penida, a 30-minute ride by boat will take you to Nusa Lembongan, the smaller and more popular sister island with beautiful beaches, turquoise water and some of the best opportunities for snorkelling in the area.

Location: irregular boats leave for Nusa Penida and Nusa Lembongan from Padangbai, taking between 2 and 3 hours. Travel agencies in Kuta and Sanur now offer package tours, and will arrange accommodation.

PADANGBAI

This charming little fishing village, although best known as the departure point for the island of Lombok, has plenty to recommend it, including fine snorkelling and boat trips to the island of Nusa Penida (2 hours), plus a host of cheap and cheerful bungalows. At night you will see the lights of the colourful fishing fleet heading out to sea and at dawn the sun rising from behind the distant hills near Mount Agung. There are now several restaurants, too, set around the crescent-shaped bay and renowned for their delicious fresh seafood.

Location: 56km north of Denpasar, off the main road to Klungkung and Amlapura. Buses run from Denpasar's Batubulan terminal. Car and passenger ferries to Lombok leave regularly throughout the day.

A shrimp fisherman sifts his way through the waters of Lovina Beach with a scissor net

The dramatic sea cliffs at Pantai Suluban, eroded by the powerful rollers treasured by the surfers

PANTAI SULUBAN (Uluwatu Beach)

Surfers flock to this magnificent spot at the base of steep cliffs to take on some of the most testing waves on the whole of the island. Most surfers bring their own boards and colourful regalia, but amateurs can hire all the equipment from nearby stalls. Beware dangerous currents though, especially at high tide, and if in doubt, just watch.

Location: 22km south of Kuta, on the Bukit Peninsula. To get to the surfing point, take the signposted path to the right, a short distance before you reach Uluwatu Temple. Motorbike drivers will take you along the 2km dirt track for a small charge – or else you can walk.

PURA ULUWATU (Uluwatu Temple)

The most staggering thing about the Uluwatu Temple is its setting on the edge of sheer cliffs overlooking the Indian Ocean. Built in the 11th century in grey volcanic stone, this revered edifice also houses a troop of monkeys known to run riot among unsuspecting tourists and locals. To appease them, buy peanuts in the nearby car park and hold on tightly to cameras, sunglasses and other valuables lest they take more of a mouthful than you bargained for. (See the Badung drive, pages 92–3.)

Location: 20km south of Kuta. Buses run from Denpasar's Tegal terminal, next to the intersection of Jalan Imam Bonjol and Jalan G Willis. For direct transport, take one of the minibuses organised by most travel agents. Open: daily, 7am–5pm. Donation requested.

TANAHLOT

Every travel agent runs trips to this 16th-century temple perched out at sea on a rocky outcrop and neither the afternoon crowds of tourists nor the markets selling over-priced trinkets can detract from the

glorious moment when its five shrines are silhouetted against the setting sun. For the best photographs, station yourself on the cliff directly opposite the temple. Early arrivals get best seats, others find their views obscured by the lines of tripods. At low tide it is possible to walk over the rocks to the temple, although access is only permitted at festival time.
Location: 31km northwest of Denpasar. Bemos run from Denpasar's Ubung terminal on Jalan Cokroaminoto to Kediri, where you must change for the 12km ride to Tanahlot. To avoid returning at night, a better alternative is to take a tour. Open: daily. Admission by donation (so long as it is more than Rp500).

TULAMBEN
If it wasn't for a US cargo boat that was torpedoed during World War II, this little village on the east coast might have remained off the beaten track for ever. However, the beaching of the ship and its cargo at Tulamben led to an influx of interest that has continued ever since. You can still see the wreck of the S S *Liberty* some 50–60m offshore and enjoy some of the finest diving on Bali here. There's not a lot else to the place, however, except black-pebbled shores, a few charming bungalows and a feeling of being remote from mainstream Bali.
Location: 27km north of Amlapura, beyond the village of Culik. Irregular bemos run from Amlapura. Better still, take your own transport.

YEH SANIH
This tranquil little spot has cool freshwater springs as well as picturesque gardens. It makes a good spot to spend the night if you are continuing further up the coast.
Location: 18km east of Singaraja. Bemos run from Singaraja's Kampung Tinggi terminal, taking 40 minutes. Nearby sites include the Pura Beji at Sangsit (10km).

The holy temple at Tanahlot

Coastal Bali

Starting out from Sanur, this drive takes you to Benoa village and from here to some of the most beautiful beaches on Bali. Along the way you will see the spectacular Uluwatu Temple, and a few other interesting sights besides. *Allow 1 day.*

Begin at Sanur Beach which lies on the east coast, some 8km from Denpasar, and take breakfast on the patio of the Hyatt – or any other hotel of your choice.

1 SANUR BEACH

For decades a charming little backwater, this bay has now been transformed into a complex of up-market hotels, leafy

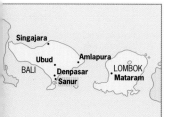

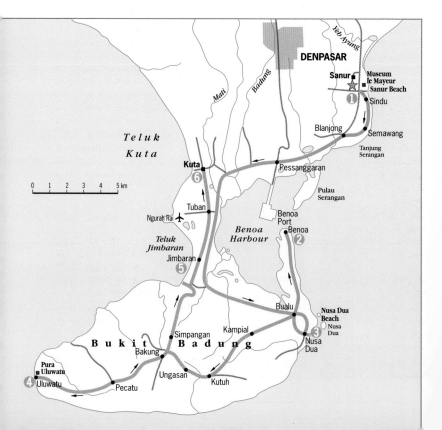

bungalows and tropical restaurants. For a reminder of the old days, visit the Museum le Mayeur next to the Bali Beach Hotel, or take a short trip out to sea in one of the local fishing boats.

From Sanur, drive 20km south on the road to Nusa Dua. Shortly before you arrive, you will see a signpost on your left for Benoa village, which lies 5km further on.

2 BENOA VILLAGE

During the late 19th century, the area around this fishing village on the Bukit Peninsula was the hunting ground for Denpasar's rajas. These days it has become popular with tourists who come here to water-ski, to paraglide or take boat trips to nearby Pulau Serangan (Turtle Island).

From Benoa village, backtrack 5km to the turn-off and follow the signpost to Nusa Dua. Park next to any of the hotels and wander down to the beach.

3 NUSA DUA

Residents of Nusa Dua swear that this vast and isolated peninsula offers the best of all worlds. It has a beautiful bay, luxurious hotels tucked away in tropical splendour – and there are no masseurs or vendors. Beware excessive eating or drinking though as prices are sky-high.

Leave Nusa Dua and keep going for 9km until you see a left-hand turning to Uluwatu. Follow the signposts for 9km until you reach Pura Uluwatu.

4 PURA ULUWATU (ULUWATU TEMPLE)

You will find this temple hanging on for dear life to a cliff that drops sheer into the sea 100m below. It's flanked by statues of Ganesh and guarded by a platoon of monkeys that bounce around with great ferocity, begging for peanuts

With its fine beaches, no wonder Sanur's inhabitants smile

and stealing cameras. Make sure you hold on to all your belongings tightly.

From Uluwatu Temple return to the main road and backtrack, following signs to Denpasar. After about 15km you will reach the village of Jimbaran.

5 JIMBARAN

At the end of a stunning stretch of road that offers fine views of the coastline is this little fishing village nestling close to a crescent of white sand and turquoise sea. So far there are only a couple of smart hotels, a temple and a few stalls here, but get here soon as big developments are planned.

Follow signs for Denpasar until you see a signpost to the left for Kuta Beach. Park anywhere near the seafront.

6 KUTA BEACH

The antithesis of Nusa Dua and Sanur, Kuta literally seethes with crowds and sheer excitement (see also pages 78–9). Take a stroll past outrageously semi-clad sun-bathers or hit the surf on a board, always making sure that it is in an area patrolled by lifeguards. Afterwards revel in the magnificent sunsets for which Kuta is renowned, but make sure that you don't leave it too late before heading back to Sanur or Denpasar.

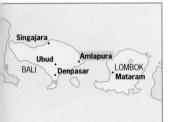

Eastern Bali

Starting out from the popular little beach resort of Candi Dasa, this pleasant drive will take you to ancient temples, magnificent rice fields and beaches. Those captivated by the scenery can even spend the night along the way. *Allow a whole day.*

Begin at the beach resort of Candi Dasa which lies on the eastern coast of Bali, a 2-hour drive from Denpasar.

1 CANDI DASA

Although it cannot compare with Kuta in terms of its beaches or its nightlife, Candi Dasa does have lots of pretty fishing boats as well as opportunities for walking and swimming. Its biggest attraction is the beautiful lagoon that lies at the eastern end of the beach.
From Candi Dasa drive north along the main road to Amlapura, which lies 13km further on.

2 AMLAPURA

Originally called Karangasem, this sleepy provincial town was renamed after it almost went up in smoke when Mount Agung erupted in 1963, killing several hundred inhabitants. To see what survived visit the 19th-century Puri Agung (Puri Kanginan) on Jalan Teuku Umar, with its sculptured panels, its dilapidated courtyard used for royal tooth-filing ceremonies and its floating pavilion.
From Puri Agung, follow the one-way system around until you re-cross the bridge at the entrance of town. Turn right for Tirtagangga, which is signposted 7km further north.

3 TIRTAGANGGA

Surrounded by some of the most staggering rice terraces in the whole of Bali, this area also plays host to the famous Tirtagangga water palace which was built in 1948 by King Gusti Bagus

and damaged 15 years later by the eruption of Mount Agung. There are shady gardens and fountains for picnickers, plus a swimming pool.
From Tirtagangga continue north for 11km until you reach the village of Culik.

4 CULIK

At the end of another fine stretch of road which winds its way past spectacular rice terraces you will reach the village of Culik, overshadowed by distant Mount Agung. Enthusiastic divers can continue straight on to the town of Tulamben (see page 91), scene of one of Bali's most famous shipwrecks.
Leave the village of Culik and turn almost immediately right to Amed, which is situated 3km further on.

5 AMED

This sleepy Muslim fishing village with its black sand and colourful fishing boats offers magnificent views of Mount Agung, especially at sunset. For a short trip out to sea, pay the locals to take you out in their boats. Those wanting to keep their feet on land can simply walk along the beach and watch salt-panners hard at work.
Continue along the road for a further 4km until you reach the small village of Bunutan.

6 BUNUTAN

This quiet fishing village is a perfect retreat from the crowds and you will find several charming places serving food and refreshments. If it's late spend the night, as the last section of the journey is the

Fishermen along the east coast

most difficult and time consuming.
From Bunutan continue for 27km along a steep, winding and poorly surfaced road until you reach Puri Taman Ujung.

7 PURI TAMAN UJUNG (UJUNG WATER PALACE)

Although little remains of the grand water palace constructed by Anak Agung Anglurah in 1921, visitors can still explore the area once graced by moats and fountains. That glorious chapter came to an end with the eruption of Mount Agung, which left only a few sculptures and portals since worn down by the wind and the rain.
From Puri Taman Ujung, continue 3km north to Amlapura from where you can retrace your steps to Candi Dasa or take the road to Selat and Besakih.

OPENING DETAILS
Puri Agung (Amlapura). Open: daily, 8am–5pm. Admission charge.

Inland Bali

*B*eyond the touristy beaches of Kuta, Sanur and Nusa Dua lies a different face of Bali, a richly textured canvas of intricate rice terraces, volcanoes and dreamy villages. Here you will discover the temples of Besakih, beautiful Danau Batur (Lake Batur) and the fast-growing cultural centre of Ubud, as well as countless other attractions which remain further off the beaten track.

Visits to these towns and sites can easily be arranged by any hotel or tour agent, but it is better to hire a jeep or a motorbike, or even a bicycle, and go where your fancy takes you.

DENPASAR

Bali's capital of 300,000 people has traffic jams, banks and shops by the dozen, but besides a museum and a colourful market few real places of interest. Visit the tourist authority on Jalan Surapati 7 (tel: 0361 22387) to get details of any festivals that are being held during your stay, and explore the shops and restaurants on Jalan Gajah Mada.

Apart from this, there is little reason to spend much time here, except perhaps to take a horse and cart around the city.

Getting There
Denpasar's Ngurah Rai International Airport, which lies 12km south of town, has connections with Europe, Asia and North America and regular flights serve all domestic destinations. Overnight buses run from major cities on Java to Ubung Terminal on Jalan Cokroaminoto and generally include the price of the ferry ticket from Ketapang to Gilimanuk. All major travel agencies will organise tickets.

Island Transport
Getting in and out of Denpasar can be a less than wonderful experience with *bemos* (minibuses) arriving and departing from several different terminals. For the west of Bali, North Bali and Java, go to the Ubung terminal on Jalan Cokroaminoto. For Sanur, go to the Kereneng terminal off Jalan Kamboja, and for the east, go to Batubulan terminal 6km to the northeast of town, near the village of Batubulan. *Bemos* also leave for Kuta, Legian and Nusa Dua

The Bali Museum complex is an amalgamation of palace and temple architecture

from the Tegal terminal, next to the intersection of Jalan Imam Bonjol and Jalan G Willis. There are also metered taxis and delightful horse-drawn carts known as *dokars* for hire.

Bali Museum
Art lovers will have a field day at the Bali Museum with its selection of pieces ranging from prehistoric times to the early 20th century. Items include fine masks, paintings and woodcarvings, along with several less easily identifiable implements. Note, too, the beautiful stone sculptures, gateways and pavilions, best seen by climbing the steps in the far corner.

Next door to the museum you will find the state temple of Pura Jagatnatha, devoted to the supreme god Sanghyang Widi, and containing a famous statue of a turtle and two *naga* snakes, symbolising the founding of the world.
Jalan Wishnu, near Puputan Square in the centre of town. Open: Tuesday to Thursday Saturday and Sunday, 8am–5pm; Friday, 8am–3pm. Admission charge.

Taman Budaya (New Arts Centre)
Most visitors bypass this delightful arts centre in their haste to get to the Bali Museum, but it offers not only paintings, sculptures and fine examples of Balinese architecture, but also lush gardens with lotus ponds. Exhibits on show include work from famous artists such as Affandi and Ida Bagus. On most evenings, there is traditional Legong or mask dancing performed by the island's famous academy of Indonesian dance on the open-air stage. Enquire locally for details.
Jalan Nusa Indah, 3km east of the Bali Museum. Open: daily, 8am–4pm. Admission charge.

Alun-Alun Puputan monument commemorates the mass suicide of Bali's nobility in 1906

ROYAL SUICIDE
When Dutch troops surrounded Denpasar's royal palace on 20 September 1906, Bali's nobility dressed up in all their finery, flung open the gates and committed mass suicide by rushing headlong at the attacking forces or stabbing each other with ceremonial knives and spears. Several hundred people died in all, and a monument has since been built in their honour, called Alun-Alun Puputan (Suicide Square).

VILLAGE CREMATION

As the midday sun beats down on the small village of Pejeng, in Central Bali, a line of villagers rushes headlong down the main street carrying great wooden towers covered in tinsel and glitter. At every intersection the wooden towers are shaken

Now that the celebrations are under way, the souls of the deceased may finally begin a new life as they are reborn in a different and possibly better form as part of the endless cycle

and spun to the sound of cheers and laughter and the music of the *gamelan*.

This festive occasion is not, however, a wedding or a temple anniversary, but a Balinese cremation for seven members of a family, some of whom died more than two years ago.

Like many families they have waited many years to save sufficient money to pay for the lavish send-off. Predictably, they have also awaited a suitably auspicious date.

of birth and death.

After the Brahman priest, or *pedanda*, has murmured prayers and placed offerings of rice and sweetmeats

to the gods, the decomposed bodies are dug up, dressed in white cloth and anointed in sweet-smelling perfume and oils. They are then given money and goods for their long journey to the next world and a sprig of jasmine flower for their nose. Finally, each body is placed in a tower, whirled around so the spirits will not be able to find their way back home, and torched by flames.

By the time dusk falls, the ashes have been taken to the nearby river, the locals are celebrating the new beginnings with rice wine, and the Balinese heavens have gained a new addition to their smiling ranks.

Far left: a decorated cremation tower
Far left (main): village funeral procession
Left: a *Gamelan* band
Top and above: burning the body

Some of Bali's finest stone carvings are found at Batubulan

AROUND DENPASAR

Dotted along the main roads that lead out of Denpasar are hundreds of little villages each specialising in a different form of artistry. Some make the most colourful shrines, others are renowned for mythical animals, carved wooden demons or even kitsch garden gnomes. *Bemos* leave from the various different terminals around the city (see pages 96–7), or, alternatively, take your own transport – but be prepared for very heavy and congested traffic around here.

Batubulan

The sound of workers chipping away on stone is the first noise you are likely to hear at Batubulan, a small town which has become famous for its stone sculpture. Here you will find rows of temple guardians, mythical animals, demons and other sculptures of every shape and size. The name Batubulan itself means 'moon stone' and the whole area offers abundant supplies of the stuff. There are also several shops sporting antiques, ceramics and woodcarvings.

Five times a week, at 10am, local dance troupes perform the *barong*, *kecak* and *kris* dances for tour groups. Be warned, however; the price of every souvenir within miles will soar sky-high until the coaches depart at around 11am, leaving the village and the workers to return to their real world.
10km northeast of Denpasar, on the road to Ubud and Gianyar.

Celuk

Best known as a prolific producer of silver, this little village sells almost every type of jewellery you can think of, and bracelets and earrings can be made to order. In some of the shops and vast air-conditioned galleries you can watch craftsmen hammering away on ornate silver and gold designs destined to be exported to Europe and Japan. Before buying, remember to shop around, as easy money has led to inflated prices.
12km northeast of Denpasar on the road to Ubud and Gianyar.

Kapal

This little village has two claims to fame. Not only is it the sculpture capital of Bali and a prolific manufacturer of shrines, but it is also home to the Pura Sada, one of the oldest temples on the island. Dating from the 12th century and set back a short distance from the main road, it was destroyed by an earthquake in 1917 and only restored in 1949. You will still find some fine stone carvings though, as well as statues of the nine lords of directions. Just in case these deities are not enough to safeguard the inhabitants from another earthquake, you will find a spirit house outside set in the midst of a huge tangled banyan tree.
12km northwest of Denpasar, on the road to Mengwi.

Lukluk

Take a left turn off the main road at the village of Lukluk to see the charming Pura Dalem Temple. You may have to ask the guardian to open the gates, but if you do you will be rewarded by fine stone carvings and pleasant leafy surroundings which you will probably have to yourself.
10km northwest of Denpasar, on the road to Mengwi.

Sukawati

Situated almost midway between Denpasar and Ubud, this bustling market town is the producer of one of Bali's most pleasing commodities – those wind chimes which tinkle in the wind, sounding like the music of the gods. There's little other reason to come here except to visit the 'Sukawati art market', a vast complex of overpriced and often poorly made handicrafts ranging from woodcarvings to *krises* and baskets made of palm leaf.
13km northeast of Denpasar, on the road to Ubud and Gianyar.

Visitors are welcome in Celuk

RAMA SITHA
SILVER
— Celuk·Gianyar·Bali —

Pura Kehen Temple near the ancient town of Bangli

AMLAPURA, see Amlapura drive, pages 94–5.

BANGLI

The highlight of this ancient little town which is situated in the cool rice fields of Central Bali is a visit to the Pura Kehen Temple with its magnificent staircase, terraced courtyards and fine stone relief carvings. Locals claim that the 11 tapering roofs and inner shrine with thrones for Brahma, Shiva and Vishnu have made it the holiest of all resting places for visiting gods. According to early inscriptions, it may have been constructed in the 9th century. It is currently under renovation, but is open daily, 8.30am–5pm.
Location: 40km northeast of Denpasar. Regular bemos *run from Denpasar's Batubulan terminal to Bangli. Pura Kehen*

is 1km north of town, on the road to Besakih and Penelokan. Donation requested.

BEDUGUL

A short drive from Bedugul will bring you to delightful Lake Bratan. Not only are there fine walks around the lakeside, speed boats and pedal boats for hire, but one of the most serene temples in the whole of Bali – Pura Ulun Danu. The temple, which is dedicated to the goddess of water, was built in 1633 by the king of Mengwi. Although it nearly sank in the mid-1970s when the waters in the lake began to rise, today it can be seen in all its simple glory. Get there at dusk to see the temple at its best and stay in one of the nearby bungalows which have panoramic views.
Location: 48km north of Denpasar. Regular

bemos _run from Denpasar's Ubung terminal on Jalan Cokroaminoto. Ask to be dropped off at Bedugul or, better still, at Lake Bratan, 2km further on. Pura Ulu Danu is open daily, 8am–4pm. Admission charge._

Bukit Mungsu (Central Market)

Flowers, vegetables and a dazzling display of spices, along with orchid seeds and occasionally even carrots, are neatly stacked up in this little market
Candikuning: 500m north of Pura Ulu Danu on the road to Bedugul.

Handara Country Club

Voted one of the world's 50 most beautiful golf courses, this impressive 18-hole course offers world-class-standard greens. Telephone 28866 for reservations.
2km north of Lake Bratan.

Kebun Raya (Botanical Gardens)

These gardens cover 130 hectares and contain more than 1,000 different trees, plants and flowers. They were established in 1959 as an offshoot of the national botanical gardens at Bogor and today are prized above all for their wild orchids.
Next to the market. Open: daily, 8am–4pm. Admission charge.

BESAKIH

When the sacred Gunung Agung (Mount Agung) volcano erupted on 17 March 1963 it literally engulfed Bali's 'mother temple', killing several hundred priests who leapt into the flames while trying to appease the angry gods. The 11th-century complex has since been rebuilt in all its magnificence, with 22 different temples spread over an area of more than 1 sq km.

For the majority of the time visitors can't actually explore Pura Agung, the most important single shrine, as regulations prohibit non-Hindus from entering the inner courtyards. Guides will, however, take you to a panoramic viewpoint from where you can see the profusion of _puras_ scattered over the slopes below. Enthusiasts can even climb Mount Agung (3,142m) from here, although you should make sure you take a guide and allow at least 5 hours to get to the summit (see Getting Away From it All, page 134).
Location: 60km northeast of Denpasar. Bemos run from Denpasar's Batubulan terminal to Klungkung. From here catch another bemo to Besakih. Open: daily, 8am–5pm. Donations requested.

Sacred temples at Besakih

Multi-tiered shrines, or *merus*, at Pura Taman Ayun, the main temple of the Mengwi kingdom

GUNUNG AGUNG (Mount Agung),
see page 134.

GUNUNG BATUR (Mount Batur)
Rising up from Lake Batur, strewn with rocks and boulders, this dramatic mountain is one of the best and most accessible peaks on Bali from where to view the sunrise. Guides can be rented at many of the bungalows and guesthouses in the small village of Kedisan, a short distance from Penelokan. (See Getting Away From it All, page 134.)

KINTAMANI
This scruffy little town offers fine views of Lake Batur below. There's little reason to stay here, however, except to visit two temples in the near vicinity.
Location: 68km north of Denpasar, beyond the town of Penelokan.

Pura Batur
When Mount Batur erupted for the second time in 1926, the locals simply dismantled what was left of the temple, moved it to safer ground near the crater rim and dedicated it to the goddess of the crater lake. The result is not only one of the island's most revered nine-tiered *merus*, but one of its most important directional temples.
A short distance south of Kintamani. Open: daily. Donation required.

Pura Tegeh Koripan
Temple buffs rank the Pura Tegeh Koripan as one of the oldest and holiest on Bali, but unless you relish the thought of climbing 300 steps, you'd be well advised to give the place a miss. At the topmost shrine are some rather ordinary-looking statues, and some portraits of Balinese kings, queens and divinities said

Intricately terraced rice fields near Pupuan in northern Bali

to date back to the 11th century.
8km north of Kintamani at the town of Penulisan. Open: daily. Donation required.

KLUNGKUNG

Until the Dutch attacked Bali's most important principality in 1908, Klung-kung was home to the powerful Gelgel dynasty and a flourishing centre for the arts. These days it is a pleasant little handicraft town best known for its royal palace and its traditional style of painting.
Location: 40km east of Denpasar. Bemos leave from Denpasar's Batubulan terminal.

Kertha Gosa

This famous little palace contains a beautiful pavilion surrounded by a moat and a hall of justice, with fine Klungkung-style paintings on the ceiling. The most vivid of them show women being boiled alive or having their heads sawn in two – the punishment for the guilty. Adjoining the court of justice is the Bale Kambang, or 'floating pavilion'. Further round, there is a small museum with ancient ceramics, paintings and a collection of weaving looms.
The Kertha Gosa lies at the main intersection on Jalan Untung Surapati. Open: daily. Admission charge.

MENGWI

This town's most popular temple, Pura Taman Ayun, has a number of impressive shrines with slender-tiered roofs as well as a pleasant courtyard surrounded by a moat filled with lotus flowers. The temple was originally constructed in the mid-18th century, but renovated in the 1930s.
Location: 18km north of Denpasar. Buses run from Denpasar's Ubung terminal. Other attractions in the vicinity: Tanah Lot (12km) and the monkey forest at Sangeh (9km).

Amlapura's ornamental gardens at Tirtagangga

PENELOKAN

From the crater rim at Penelokan it is easy to see why the locals call Bali the island of gods, for the views that can be had of Mount Batur and the turquoise lake below are among the finest on offer. There are plenty of other attractions within easy reach, too. While enthusiastic walkers leave every morning to climb the peak of Mount Batur, less energetic individuals simply relax by the lake in the village of Kedisan (4km).

Location: 60km north of Denpasar. Bemos run from Denpasar's Batubulan terminal to Bangli, from where you must catch another bemo for Penelokan. There is also a regular coach service. For the best places to stay, take the road east to Kedisan (4km).

PUPUAN

The real joy of visiting Pupuan is the journey there through spectacular rice terraces with distant views of Gunung Batukau (Mount Batukau). For a pleasant day's excursion, take the winding route from Seririt (west of Singaraja) or travel all the way north from Pulukan, but whichever way you

go, take your time. This is a journey for connoisseurs, and if you are in a hurry, don't even dream of it.

Location: 42km southwest of Singaraja. Buses occasionally travel the road, but it is best appreciated with your own transport.

SANGEH

An intrepid band of monkeys inhabits this sacred temple (Pura Bukit Sari) and the surrounding forest planted with nutmeg trees. Bring a camera and a handful of peanuts, but hold on tight to all your belongings.

Location: 9km northeast of Mengwi, via the town of Kedampal. Use private transport.

SINGARAJA

When the Dutch occupied northern Bali in the 19th century, they chose this little town as their capital. Although most tourists now hurry through on their way to the beaches of Lovina, you will still find a handful of old colonial buildings on Jalan Ngurah Rai as well as tree-lined avenues and rows of Chinese shops.

Location: 78km north of Denpasar. Regular buses leave from Kuta Beach and from Denpasar. Bemos leave from Denpasar's Ubung terminal on Jalan Cokroaminoto.

Pura Beji

This delightful little temple has a fine gateway of *naga* snakes and some of the most detailed stone carvings on Bali. It is built in the northern style and dedicated to the goddess of agriculture.

7km east of Singaraja in the village of Sangsit.

TENGANAN

A brand new stretch of road leads through lush countryside to this Bali Aga village, home to some original Balinese and to a host of colourful customs,

boxing contests and mating dances dating back hundreds of years. However, the real world has arrived in this beautiful little village with a vengeance. Outside the courtyard, with its rows of diminutive houses and stalls selling famous Ikat cloth made from silk, woven and dyed by hand, there is now a car park large enough to handle coach tours and inside the village one of the first things you see is a concrete public convenience.
Location: 4km north of Candi Dasa. Motorbike taxis will take you from the signposted turn-off. Donation requested.

TIRTAGANGGA

Many visitors travel to Tirtagangga simply to admire the rice terraces, but the place has another attraction: the water

Bali Aga woman, Tenganan

Fine stone carvings at Pura Beji, Singaraja

palace built by Amlapura's last raja which features fountains, ornamental gardens and a swimming pool. Locals come here with picnics and sit on the green lawns. Tourists can take their pick of several restaurants, including an Indian curry house. (See the Amlapura drive, page 94.)
Location: 85km from Denpasar. Bemos run via the town of Amlapura. The water palace is open daily. Admission charge.

TRUNYAN

Unless you relish the idea of being hassled by some of the pushiest inhabitants on the whole of Bali, you'd be well advised to stay clear of this Bali Aga village, which is inhabited by descendants of the original Balinese. The only real attractions of the place are a 4m-high statue of a guardian spirit and a cemetery where the people are left to decompose.
Location: catch a fixed-price boat from the village of Kedisan, 4km east of Penelokan, which will take you on a round-trip to Trunyan. Boats leave daily at regular intervals between 8.30am and 3.30pm.

RICE FARMING

In the beautiful heartlands that make up Central Bali, the first light of day reveals farmers already out in their lush paddy fields, knee-deep among the glistening green shoots that stretch to a distant horizon.

Some of these people have worked in the fields for an entire lifetime, others only do so during the harvest, but almost everyone on this fertile island in some way contributes to the annual crop of rice which exceeds 900,000 tons.

Nor is it only Bali where the production of rice is the single most important commodity. Almost four out of five Javanese work the soil, each consuming an average of 180kg of rice every year and making Java both one of the biggest producers and consumers in the world. Even on Lombok, around the delightful village of Tetebatu, you will see workers thrashing out husks beneath the shadow of Mount Rinjani.

Generally the rice is planted by hand and the terraced paddies are then flooded by a complex system of irrigation channels leading from nearby rivers and streams. Within a matter of weeks the young green shoots appear. As soon as the rice has ripened and turned to a golden brown, men and

women from the surrounding area gather to cut the crop, remove the husks and store the grain to feed their families in the months to come.

Far left: rice fields at Pupuan
Left: central Bali
Bottom left: planting the rice seedlings
Above: terraces in northern Bali
Below: harvesting the crop

In the past the harvest benefited from the extremely rich volcanic soil, with farmers often harvesting two crops a year. With the introduction of new high yield, insect-resistant strains, however, the output will soon be even higher and the rice gods recipients of even greater praise.

UBUD

This delightful town surrounded by rice fields is undoubtedly the most popular inland destination on Bali as well as the most rewarding. Ubud is not only cooler than the coastal areas, but has a wealth of cultural activities and opportunities for walking, shopping or just relaxing. You can feast on *babi guling* (roasted pig), shop for paintings and woodcarvings, or take gentle strolls in the surrounding countryside. Ubud also makes the perfect stepping-stone for trips to the north.
Location: 25km north of Denpasar. Tourist buses run from Kuta and Sanur to Ubud. Bemos *run from Denpasar's Batubulan terminal, taking 1 hour.*

Orientation

There are only two roads of any significance in Ubud. Running east to west you'll find Jalan Raya, where the central market and dozens of shops and restaurants are located; running north to south is Monkey Forest Road, with art shops, stalls and charming little bungalows. Good restaurants and a range of accommodation can be found everywhere, so just wander until you find something that takes your fancy.

Museum Neka

A fine collection of paintings ranging from work by famous local artists such as Ida Bagus and Anak Agung to collections by western artists which include Le Mayeur, Walter Spies and Antonio Blanco is on display at this museum. Set up in 1982 by Suteja Neka, it provides a wonderful insight into the transition from traditional to modern Balinese style. Paintings by local artists are in the first gallery arranged in chronological order. To see paintings by Western artists, visit the second and third galleries.
1.5km west of Ubud past the village of Campuhan. Open: daily, 9am–noon and 2pm–5pm. Admission charge.

Museum Puri Lukisan (Palace of Fine Arts)

This little museum is a must for anyone interested in the development of modern art on Bali. Set up in the mid 1950s, it

The rice fields of Ubud

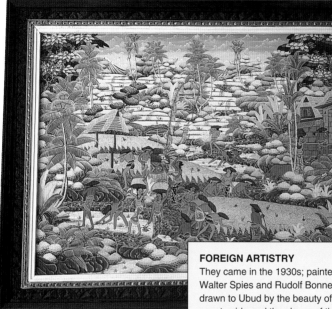

Ubud's paintings combine traditional subjects with a modern style of artistry

has an excellent display of paintings and sculptures, and an idyllic little garden. *Jalan Raya, just west of the market. Open: daily, 8am–4pm. Admission charge.*

FOREIGN ARTISTRY

They came in the 1930s; painters like Walter Spies and Rudolf Bonnet, drawn to Ubud by the beauty of the countryside and the charm of the people. Over the years they were joined by a host of other local and foreign artists. And the result? An intriguing mix of styles and colours that provides yet a new perspective on the island, its religions and its inhabitants.

Shopping

Art galleries, studios and souvenir stalls have sprung up all over Ubud, selling every form of painting, antique or wooden carving imaginable, as well as a host of shirts and tie-dye bed covers. Some of them are real artistic pieces, but most are mass produced.

Temples and Shrines

Several temples can be found along Jalan Raya, including the Pura Saren and the delightful Puri Saraswati, situated behind the Lotus Café Restaurant. For other temples and countless shrines, just keep your eyes open – you won't be able to miss them.

Wayang Kulit and Dances

If you haven't already seen the Wayang Kulit shadow puppets or the mask dance, or even the Legong and Kecak dance, Ubud is the place to put this right. Performances take place almost every night either at the Pura Dalem or the Puri Saren. Check your guesthouse for details, and get there early to reserve a seat.

UBUD

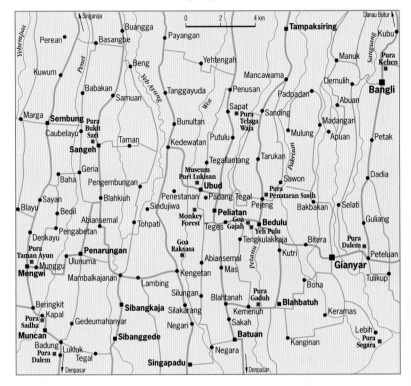

AROUND UBUD

For a glimpse of handicrafts and beautiful countryside, go to any of these villages which lie within a 10km radius of Ubud. Most of them can be reached by *bemos* which leave regularly from the market place on the corner of Monkey Forest Road and Jalan Raya. Alternatively, just walk out into the countryside and make up your own route. You're unlikely to be disappointed.

Batuan

Some of Bali's finest ink drawings are to be found in this village, along with plenty of second-rate imitations. Much of the work is said to be influenced by the great Made Nyana who was born here in 1948, while other paintings are by Nyoman Lempad. You may find the Batuan style to be moodier than the Ubud style, but purists claim it to be just as good.

7km south of Ubud.

Bedulu

This little village might have gone by an altogether different name if it hadn't

been for the ability of a former king with two heads to switch them at will, which led to the term Bedulu (he who changed heads). Walk east of the junction to see the town's most important site, the Pura Samuan Tiga. It was built in the 11th century when the town was capital of the Pejeng kingdom, and every year, on the full moon of the tenth month, hosts one of the island's most important festivals, Odalan.
5km east of Ubud.

Campuan

This little village, which was once the proud home of Dutch artist Arie Smit, still plays host to American artist Antonio Blanco, as well as several delightful *losmen* (bungalows) and the charming Hotel Tjampuhan, former home of artist Walter Spies. Leave the main road to enjoy beautiful strolls in the

Stone demons perched over the town of Gianyar

rice fields.
1km west of Ubud (see the Ubud to Campuan walk, pages 118–9).

Gianyar

You would be hard pushed to spend more than a morning in this bustling modern town, renowned for its textiles and its *babi guling* (roast pig). Having said this, you can visit the factories to watch sarongs being woven and catch a glimpse of the old palace of the Gianyar royal family, which is a fine example of traditional Balinese architecture. The palace on Jalan Ngurah Rai is still inhabited though, so you can only inspect it from the outside.
10km southeast of Ubud.

Carvings at Pura Samuan Tiga (Temple of the Meeting of the Three), Bedulu

Goa Gajah

A fantastically carved rock and a cave full of phallic symbols are the chief attractions of this popular tourist site which lies a short distance from Ubud. You can explore the dimly lit interior of this 11th-century hermitage, although you must walk through the mouth of a Kala head to enter. Inside is a statue of the elephant-headed god Ganesh, as well as various symbols of the Hindu god Shiva. Excavations outside the cave have also uncovered two bathing pools with six statues of nymphs holding waterspouts.

4km east of Ubud. Open: daily. Admission charge. Most trips combine Goa Gajah with a visit to nearby Yeh Pulu (1km).

Jalan Monkey Forest (Monkey Forest Road), see the Ubud to Nyuh Kuning walk, pages 116–17.

Mas

Shrewd art collectors have been visiting this village for decades to get their hands on the beautiful wooden carvings, including fruit bowls and mythical birds, which are displayed in its galleries. These

Mas has a high reputation for producing quality carvings and masks

days they are accompanied by a wealthier and less discerning clientele with the result that some of the most intricate woodcarvings on Bali lie alongside some of the nastiest and most expensive examples. Check out several of the showrooms, and remember that the smarter the place, the higher the prices.

4km south of Ubud. Showrooms generally open 8.30am–4.30pm. Admission free.

Pejeng

A vast drum measuring over 3m long is the highlight of Pejeng's old state temple known as Pura Panataran Sasih. Legend tells that this was formerly the thirteenth moon which fell to earth when a thief urinated on it. Nearby temples have equally catching names and stories. You'll find the 14th-century Pura Pusering Jagat (Navel of the World) a short distance south and next door the Pura Kebo Edan (Crazy Buffalo Temple) with a demonic statue bearing six penises.

4km east of Ubud.

Wooden carvings can be made to order by the artisans of Mas

In the late afternoon Petulu is suddenly inundated with white egrets returning from a day's feeding

Peliatan

Peliatan's biggest claim to fame is that it plays host to one of Bali's best-known dance troupes, which performs regularly at the Puri Agung and the Pura Dalem Puri in Peliatan. So highly thought of was the troupe that during the 1950s they were used in a Hollywood film co-starring Bing Crosby and Bob Hope. Check out times at the tourist office on Jalan Raya.

1.5km southeast of Ubud.

Petulu

Although you will find plenty of proficient woodcarvers in the vicinity, this small village is above all associated with white egrets which come in their thousands to nest in the surrounding trees for much of the year. In the late afternoon photographers with powerful lenses can have a field day, but watch out for bird droppings, which can be quite prolific.

4km northeast of Ubud. Turn left where you see a sign with a large heron.

Tampaksiring

Travel north of Pejeng village to see the monumental hermitage known as Gunung Kawi set in a deep ravine and surrounded by spectacular rice terraces. The memorial shrines carved into the rock face are believed to honour an 11th-century royal family and their concubines. Other sites in the vicinity include the famous springs of Tirta Empul, 2km further north.

15km north of Ubud. Turn right on the outskirts of Tampaksiring. Open: daily. Admission charge.

Yeh Pulu

According to legend, Kebo Iwa, the great giant, carved these 14th-century rock carvings in one night with his fingernails. You will find other attractions about the place too, with its nearby rice fields and sacred well. Best to combine a trip to Yeh Pulu with a visit to nearby Goa Gajah.

Signposted 1.5km southeast of Goa Gajah.

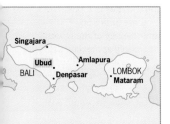

Ubud to Nyuh Kuning

Starting at the charming little gallery of Gusti Nyoman Lempad, this popular walk takes you past the central market down bustling Monkey Forest Road to the Pura Dalem Temple. From here it is a pleasant amble to the village of Nyuh Kuning. *Allow 2 hours.*

The walk begins at Gusti Nyoman Lempad's gallery on Jalan Raya.

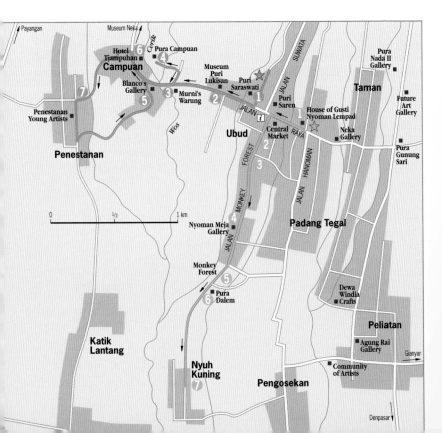

1 HOUSE OF GUSTI NYOMAN LEMPAD

This little red-brick gallery which is open to the public was formerly home to one of Bali's best-known artists, Gusti Nyoman Lempad, who died in 1978. He was responsible for a fine collection of ink drawings as well as stone carvings and Barong heads.

Leave the gallery and turn right. A short distance further along you will see the central market.

2 CENTRAL MARKET

The best time to see Ubud's main vegetable and food market is at dawn when the place is packed with locals buying exotic fruits and meats. At other times, visit the small spirit shrines next door with their clutch of offerings and joss sticks.

Leave the market and continue along Jalan Raya. After a short distance, turn left down Jalan Monkey Forest.

3 JALAN MONKEY FOREST (MONKEY FOREST ROAD)

Five years ago rice fields stretched out on both sides of Monkey Forest Road. These days they have been replaced by silversmiths, galleries and stalls selling hand-woven cottons, batiks, paintings and woodcarvings. Walk in and inspect any of the goods, but remember that the prices on Monkey Forest Road may be a little higher than in the villages outside Ubud.

Continue down Monkey Forest Road for about 800m and on your right, just before you descend the hill, you will see the gallery of Nyoman Meja.

4 NYOMAN MEJA GALLERY

This spacious gallery contains pictures by Nyoman Meja who is famous for painting traditional scenes in a post-modern style. You are under no obligation to purchase any of the works, but you should certainly appreciate them.

Continue to the entrance of the Monkey Forest 150m further on, sign your name in the book, and leave a donation. Rp500 should suffice, although the people will press you to give more.

5 MONKEY FOREST

This small but dense forest is inhabited by a band of exuberant monkeys who hang out high up in the trees, swinging from branch to branch and leaping around in search of food. Keep your hands on your cameras, sunglasses or any other valuables since they have become famous for taking more than just bananas or peanuts.

From the ticket office follow the path into the forest and on your left, after about 100m, you will find the Pura Dalem.

6 PURA DALEM (TEMPLE OF THE DEAD)

You will find this forest temple poking out of lush vegetation and over-run with monkeys. Keep your eyes open at the entrance of the inner temple for the stone carvings of *rangda* figures devouring children.

Continue down the steps to the right of the temple and follow the path. After 400m you will reach Nyuh Kuning village.

7 NYUH KUNING

This little village set amidst rice fields makes a perfect end to the tour, with its friendly woodcarvers and delightfully unhurried air of days gone by.

From Nyuh Kuning, you can either head east to Pengosekan, where there is a community of artists, or retrace your steps back to Ubud.

Ubud to Campuan

Starting out from the delightful little Saraswati temple near the centre of Ubud, this walk will take you to the Museum Puri Lukisan and from there to the surrounding villages where a number of great artists settled down to enjoy a taste of paradise. For the route see the Ubud to Nyuh Kuning walk map on page 116. *Allow 3 hours.*

Begin at the Puri Saraswati on Jalan Raya, situated behind the Lotus Café.

1 PURI SARASWATI

This little temple situated behind a lotus pond contains several fine stone carvings by the famous local artist Gusti Nyoman Lempad, as well as a magnificent stone lotus throne which is upheld as one of Ubud's great examples of artistry. Before entering, make sure you put a sash around your waist and leave a small donation.
Continue a short distance west down Jalan Raya. On your right, you will see a signpost for the Museum Puri Lukisan.

2 MUSEUM PURI LUKISAN

Built by the Noble Aspiration Foundation, which was founded by the late King of Ubud together with German artist Walter Spies and Dutch artist Rudolf Bonnet, this charming museum contains traditional and modern paintings along with a collection of wooden carvings (open: daily, 8am–4pm).
From Puri Lukisan continue west down Jalan Raya towards the village of Campuan.

3 CAMPUAN VILLAGE

Marking the spot where the Wos and

Cerik rivers converge, Campuan is a bustling little village that has become closely associated with foreign artists like Antonio Blanco and Walter Spies. You will find several craft shops, the popular Murni's Warung and, near by, pleasant walks into the rice fields.

A hundred metres before you reach the bridge follow a sign to your right for Pura Campuan and descend the steps to the temple.

4 PURA CAMPUAN (GUNUNG LEBAH)

This secluded little temple, which lies far below the bridge, is thought to date back as far as the 8th or 9th century, although it has since been thoroughly renovated. Near by is a cave believed to play host to Goa Raksasa, a local devil.

Retrace your steps to the junction and after crossing the suspension bridge over the Wos River you will find Blanco's Gallery signposted immediately on your left.

5 BLANCO'S GALLERY

This delightful edifice, set in magnificent gardens, is home to American artist Antonio Blanco who has resided here for more than 40 years. While most Balinese artists concentrate on brightly coloured rural scenes, Blanco's speciality is erotic art. If you are lucky, you may even find the great artist at work.

Continue 150m up the road and on the right you will see Hotel Tjampuhan.

6 HOTEL TJAMPUHAN

Until 1944 this exquisite establishment overlooking the river was the residence of Walter Spies, one of the European painters who settled on the island. It is now a hotel, but you can still wander in the exotic gardens and for a fee use the swimming pool.

Above and far left: the secluded temple of Pura Campuan

From Hotel Tjampuhan, walk 100m further up the road and turn left up the stone steps, signposted to Penestanan Bungalows. After following the path through rice fields for about 800m you will reach the village of Penestanan.

7 PENESTANAN

This little village has thrived as the centre of a native art movement which was inspired by the Dutch artist Arie Smit in the 1950s. Today it is full of galleries, bead centres and silver workshops as well as some delightful houses. Watch the artists at work and remember to bargain hard if you buy anything.

From Penestanan follow the road around until you arrive back at the suspension bridge. From here, it is a short walk back to Ubud.

Lombok

*O*nly a 4-hour journey away from Bali in distance, yet a decade away in development, the island of Lombok remains an oasis of calm lapped by the warm waters of the Indian Ocean.

In this newly discovered tourist destination, that measures 80km by 70km, you'll find every kind of scenery from the vast arid landscape of the south to the lush rice fields of Tetebatu and the magnificent beaches and islands that dot the western coast.

Historically, too, this is a world of contrasting cultures. During the 17th century armies from East Bali invaded Lombok, seizing many of its coastal towns from the ethnic Sasaks. Even today, although the majority of the island's 2.3 million population are Muslim, some 80,000 Balinese still live in the western districts, holding ceremonies and festivals to honour the gods.

Don't expect to find another Bali though. Lombok may have rice terraces that match those in Ubud, as well as an unspoiled coastline, but it is poorer than its eastern neighbour and does not have the serene, sweet-smiling inhabitants, nor the rich artistry and the countless temple festivities and celebrations.

For a short tour, most visitors head straight to up-market Senggigi Beach or the gem-like islands of Gili Air and Gili Trawangan. Better, though, to take your

Lombok's most spectacular landmark: Mount Rinjani viewed from Tetebatu

LOMBOK

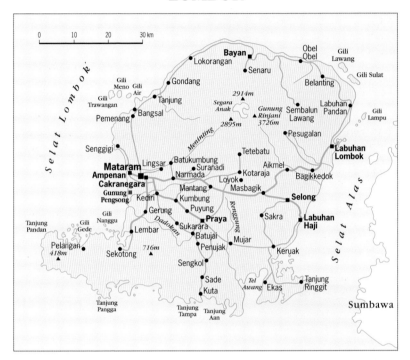

time and enjoy while you can the quieter charms of what will undoubtedly become Indonesia's next major tourist destination.

Getting There
Regular flights leave from Denpasar's Ngurah Rai Airport for Selaparang Mataram Airport on Lombok. There is also a ferry service which runs regularly from Padangbai to Lembar, taking between 4 and 5 hours, depending on the weather. Recently, a hydrofoil was introduced. It leaves Benoa Harbour every morning, arriving in Lembar 1.5 hours later.

Travelling Around
Although the Balinese will tell you that transport is undeveloped and dangerous, roads on Lombok are for the most part of an extremely good standard and, with the recent completion of a road link on the northeast coast, you can now drive right around the island. Countless visitors rent jeeps and motorbikes on Bali and transport them over on the ferry from Padangbai. Those without their own transport can take crowded public *bemos* or charter their own. For shorter trips, there is the ubiquitous horse and cart, known as a *dokar.*

MAJOR TOWNS

Lombok's three major towns lie on the west coast, a short distance from one another. Few tourists stay here, but there are a couple of sites to visit, as well as the main transportation hub at the Sweta bus terminal, 2km east of Cakranegara.

MATARAM

There is precious little reason to spend time in Lombok's capital unless it is the Bank of Indonesia or the immigration office that you are after. Besides these and a few other government offices, the place is simply a modern administrative town with an airport and a couple of rather ordinary hotels.

Location: west of Lombok. Regular bemos (minibuses) travel the short distance between Mataram, Ampenan, Cakranegara and the main bus station at Sweta, a short distance further east.

AMPENAN

A delightful way to explore this dilapidated old fishing town is to catch one of the popular bell-jingling horse and carts known as *dokars* which potter around town. Ask the driver to take you to see some of the local antique shops. A pleasant side trip can be made to the Provincial Museum of Nusa Tenggara Barat, on Jalan Banjar Tilar Negara (open: Tuesday to Thursday and Sunday, 8am–2pm; Friday, 8am–11am, Saturday, 8am–1pm), which contains a collection of textiles from around the region. Keep your eyes open for the few old Dutch buildings still remaining, and for the small but lively Chinese and Arab quarters. (See the Lombok coastal drive, pages 130–1.)

Location: 3km west of Mataram.

CAKRANEGARA

You may be hard pushed to find the exact point where Mataram ends and Cakranegara begins, but the latter is considerably busier than its neighbour, if somewhat lacking in charm. During the 17th century Cakranegara was the capital of Lombok. Today there are plenty of shops selling sarongs, baskets and silver trinkets, especially around the bazaar on Jalan Selaparang. Also keep your eyes open for stalls dispensing Lombok's gastronomic delicacy known as *ayam taliwang*, a delicious, if incongruous, flattened and heavily spiced barbecued chicken.

Location: 1km east of Mataram.

Mayura Water Palace

Built in 1744 as part of the former Balinese empire on Lombok, this palace

The Mayura Water Palace was once the hub of Cakranegara

Balinese-style temples are a feature of Lombok's Pura Meru

marks the spot where, a century later, the Balinese routed the Dutch army. You will find several old cannons as well as a delightful little shrine to the east. In the middle of the lake is an open-sided hall of justice, known as the floating pavilion. *North of Jalan Selaparang. Open: daily, 8am–5pm. Admission charge.*

Pura Meru (Meru Temple)

Cross the street from the Mayura Water Palace to see Pura Meru, which is one of the largest Balinese temples on Lombok. Prince Agung Made Karang built it in 1720 as an attempt to unify the island. Although his efforts failed, the temple, with its three courtyards and 33 shrines, lives on – dedicated to the Hindu trinity of Shiva, Brahma and Vishnu.
East of the Mayura Water Palace, off Jalan Selaparang. Open: daily, 8am–5pm. Admission charge.

Gunung Pengsong

Three hundred metres and an awful lot of steps up the hillside have to be tackled to reach this little temple shrine commanding magnificent views. At the end of March or April, locals sacrifice a water buffalo here to celebrate the end of the harvest. At other times, it is a place for die-hard fitness fanatics and those with an appreciation of fine vistas.
9km south of Mataram. Charter a bemo and ask the caretaker to open the gates. Donations appreciated.

SWEET REVENGE

When the Dutch demanded payment from Lombok in 1882, the occupying Balinese armies simply attacked their forces, killing 100 soldiers. The Dutch responded by calling up reinforcements and, supported by the Sasaks, captured Cakranegara in 1894. Shortly afterwards the island formally became a part of the Dutch East Indies.

REST OF LOMBOK

GILI ISLANDS

The three little island pearls known as Gili Trawangan, Gili Air and Gili Meno, all with magnificent beaches, fine coral and dazzling turquoise seas, lie 30 minutes away by boat off Lombok's northwest coast. There are no big hotels here, but plenty of travellers nevertheless come here to laze away the days, to feast on freshly caught fish and to watch wonderful sunsets over Gunung Agung (Mount Agung) on Bali and sunrises over Gunung Rinjani (Mount Rinjani). For the best snorkelling and the liveliest entertainment go to Gili Trawangan, and for a quieter alternative, to Gili Air. Note, however, that during high season (June–September) accommodation can be extremely hard to come by, especially if you arrive in the late afternoon.

Location: Bangsal, the departure point for the Gili Islands, lies 25km north of Ampenan and can be reached by bemo *via Pemenang. Public boats leave at irregular intervals for the islands, taking 30–45 minutes. Failing that, charter a boat.*

Around Gili

Continue further up the coast from Pemenang to beautiful Tanjung Sirah. Currently there is nowhere to stay, but you will find good snorkelling opportunities and it is one of the most tranquil spots on the island.

3km north of Pemenang.

GUNUNG RINJANI (Mount Rinjani)

Unless you hire a guide and are in reasonably good physical shape, you would be ill advised to climb this magnificent mountain. During the dry season, however, you can catch fantastic views of the summit (3,726m), typically shrouded in mist and towering over the entire island. Its enormous crater, reached by a difficult 2-day trek from the town of Bayan, is filled with emerald-green water and its steep slopes covered in forest. Twice a year the Balinese make a pilgrimage here to throw offerings to the goddess of the mountain. For the rest of the year, it remains quiet and

Bangsal is the departure point for the Gili Islands

unspoiled and indescribably beautiful.
You will experience some of the finest
views, without the effort, from the village
of Tetebatu (see pages 128–9) and from
the Gili Islands (see page 124), but from
almost anywhere on the island this
awesome mountain is visible.

*Location: northern Lombok. Best approaches
are from the town of Bayan to the north or
Sembulan Lawang to the east. (See Getting
Away From it All, pages 134–5.)*

KUTA BEACH

Don't muddle the name of this beautiful
stretch of beach with the crowded sands
of its namesake on Bali, for, despite plans
to develop this coastline into a luxury
Nusa Dua-type destination, the place still
remains largely off the beaten track. Here
backpackers mingle with fishermen and
locals against a backdrop of simple
bungalows nestling a short distance from
the sea front. Only when the winds are
high and large amounts of stinging
seaweed have been washed ashore does
the place lose some of its inherent
charms.

*Location: 60km south of Mataram. Public
bemos run from Sweta's terminal to Praya,*

Irregular and crowded ferry boats convey
visitors to and from the Gili Islands

*where you have to catch another bemo to
Sengkol and change again for Kuta. A
simpler alternative is to take your own
transport.*

Excursions from Kuta

For a pleasant excursion, head 1.5km east
to Segara Beach and take a signposted
right turn over the bridge. From the top
of the nearby hill you will get fine views of
Mount Rinjani and a series of bays.
Continue a further 3km along the main
road to the beach at Tanjung Aan, but get
here soon though, as even in this tranquil
area the talk is of new hotels and big
exclusive developments.

Kuta Market

Kuta's Sunday beach market is a sensory
delight of exotic fruits, live chickens,
woven baskets and smiling locals – and
well worth an excursion, even if beaches
are not your thing. Arrive early and be
sure to have a camera handy and vast
amounts of film.

Kuta Beach. Sundays only.

LOVE BITES

On the nineteenth day of the tenth
month of the Sasak lunar calendar
(February or March), crowds of
Sasaks head out to sea off Kuta
Beach in search of the innocuous
sea worms called Nyale fish. Legend
has it that these worms represent
the hair of the princess Nyale and
when consumed will bring ever-
lasting love and happiness. The
locals scoop them up and eat them
raw.

Guarding the shrine at Lingsar, sacred to both the Hindu and Islamic religions

Location: 15km east of Mataram. Open: daily, 8am–6pm. Admission charge. Bemos *run from the Sweta bus terminal in Cakranegara to Narmada, where you must catch another* bemo *to Lingsar.*

NARMADA

When King Anak Gede Karangasem of Mataram was too frail to climb to the summit of Mount Rinjani, he simply built an imitation of the lake and made offerings to the gods from his luxuriant gardens instead. Besides a pool which is open to the public and a small Hindu Balinese temple built in 1805, the place is run down now, with few real attractions.

Location: 10km east of Cakranegara. Bemos *run from Cakranegara's Sweta terminal. Open: daily, 8am–6pm. Admission charge.*

PENUJAK

Water pots and storage jars made from coils of clay are the speciality of this little village, situated a short distance from Praya. There is a promotion centre and plenty of locals prepared both to show off and sell their work.

Location: 5km south of Praya on the road to

LEMBAR

Lombok's main port is little more than an arrival and departure point for ferries to Bali. You will be met by dozens of *bemos* which will transport you to Ampenan, Mataram, Cakranegara and the Sweta bus terminal for onward connections.

Location: 22km south of Mataram.

LINGSAR

Legend has it that when the Balinese first arrived on Lombok, a holy spring gushed out of the earth at Lingsar. Four Hindu shrines mark the spot along with a Muslim shrine, and in the adjacent Wektu Telu temple there are numerous baby eels. From stalls in the car park buy a hard-boiled egg to feed the sacred creatures, although you will have to break it in half as the fishes' spiritual skills do not extend to swallowing the egg yolks whole.

TERRACOTTA AHOY

When travelling around Lombok keep your eyes open for the beautiful terracotta pots made by Sasak potters. These beautiful storage jars, water jugs and vases are sculptured by hand, dried in the sun and fired in open-air kilns. They can be bought all over the island.

Above: the rarely visited gardens at Narmada
Right: Sasak traditions in Sade. Other Sasak
villages in the area are less changed by tourism

Kuta. Take a bemo *from Praya. Also
included on many day tours.*

SADE

For a glimpse of traditional Sasak life,
visit this delightful little village set
incongruously between rice fields and a
tarmacked main road, a short distance
from Kuta. Be prepared though for a
barrage of women selling woven rugs and
girls as young as five demonstrating the
art of weaving. English-speaking guides
will explain the various Sasak rituals,
point you in the best direction for taking
photographs and negotiate for purchases.
Get here early to avoid the crowds.
*Location: 6km north of Kuta and included
on many day tours. A donation is requested
on entry to the village.*

SENGGIGI BEACH

Lombok's best-known beaches cannot compare with those at Nusa Dua or Sanur, but they do offer sheltered bays for swimming, white sands and, further up the coast, magnificent countryside with palm trees and rugged cliffs. Until a few years ago you might have found yourself almost entirely alone here, but these days luxury hotels (including a Sheraton) and bungalows are springing up everywhere and there are even plans for a Holiday Inn. During the day most people lie out on the beaches or relax by hotel swimming pools and in the late afternoon crowds gather by the nearby temple of Batu Bolong (see the Lombok coastal drive, pages 130–1) to watch the sunset.

Location: Senggigi Beach covers an area 12–18km north of Mataram. Bemos run from Jalan Salah Singkar in Ampenan to Senggigi, taking 40 minutes. Occasionally, you may be able to charter a bemo at Lembar.

SUKARARA

Don't be surprised to find hundreds of weavers in this little Sasak town, for Sukarara has established a reputation for producing some of the best hand-woven cloth in the area. Watch the people weaving patterned sarongs and exquisite *kain songket,* a richly coloured cloth interwoven with gold thread. For a price you can even buy woven bags, although they may be cheaper in the market in Cakranegara. If you have the time, explore the surrounding countryside with its thatched villages, its rice fields and its merry inhabitants trotting around in horse-carts.

Location: 26km south of Mataram, off the Kediri to Praya Road. Catch a bemo to Puyung and hire a dokar (horse and cart).

SURANADI

Whilst in a trance, a fervent Hindu saint supposedly founded this little village in the foothills east of Mataram and to celebrate the great event a Balinese temple was built at the source of a mountain spring. Inside the Pura Suranadi are some ornate carvings, several mischievous monkeys and lots of exceedingly holy eels. You can take walks in the vicinity and admire fine views of the hills and rice fields. Visitors wanting a longer stay can reside in a comfortable hotel with a restaurant and swimming pool opposite the temple.

Location: 18km east of Mataram. Bemos run from the Sweta bus terminal in Cakranegara to Narmada, from where you must take another bemo to Suranadi.

TETEBATU

This mountain retreat at the foot of Gunung Rinjani is the place to relax amid tropical rice fields. There are expansive views over southern Lombok as well as fine walks to the surrounding waterfalls and forests. Self-appointed guides will lead you through the rice fields to small Sasak communities, or simply get a map and go yourself. Make sure you get up early though as by lunchtime the mountain has generally clouded over and the village is covered in a thin veil of mist.

Location: 50km east of Mataram. Bemos depart from Cakranegara's Sweta terminal to the town of Pomotong, from where you must take a bemo *to Kotaraja and then another* bemo *or* dokar *to Tetebatu. Better to use your own transport.*

Excursions

Almost everyone who stays in Tetebatu will visit the beautiful Jekut waterfalls situated in the Mount Rinjani National Park, 6km east of town. Either hire a guide for the pleasant 5-hour walk there and back, or follow the road and ask directions at the entrance to the park. Make sure you take water to drink and swimming clothes. Other villages in the vicinity include Kotaraja (4km), Loyok (8km) and Pomotong (12km). Alternatively, follow any of the roads out of Tetebatu and admire some of Lombok's most magnificent countryside.

Children from the rural community of Suranadi

Lombok Coastal Drive

Starting out from the run-down old fishing port of Ampenan, this drive takes you along the beautiful coast to Bangsal and to the tranquil Gili Islands. Spend a day relaxing on Gili Air or take the circular route back via panoramic Baun Pusak. *Allow one day.*

Begin in the town of Ampenan on the west coast of Lombok, a short distance from Mataram.

1 AMPENAN

This old port was once the commercial heart of Lombok and still offers small markets, dusty alleyways and colourful fishing boats as a reminder of happier days. On Jalan Yos Sudarso you will find a Chinese quarter, and further to the north an intriguing little Arab quarter.

From Ampenan take the coastal road which heads north to Senggigi. After 1km, turn left down the small alley next to Dewi Sri Murni Tours. Pura Segara lies 0.5km further on.

2 PURA SEGARA

This little beachside temple looks as if it has come straight out of Bali, with its spirit houses, shrines and joss sticks, but the colourful fishing boats, the decayed shacks and the shy inhabitants are all Lombok.

From Pura Segara, return to the main road and continue north for 7km along the coast. Shortly before you reach Senggigi you will find the Batu Bolong temple situated on a small headland to your left.

3 BATU BOLONG

If you had come to this temple a century ago you might have seen beautiful

Spectacular views over Bangsal from the island of Gili Air

virgins being thrown into the water as offerings for the gods. These days there is only a large hole in the rock (presumably through which they leapt) and the temple jutting out to sea from where there are fine views, especially at sunset.

From Batu Bolong, continue 2km north to Senggigi Beach. You can park outside any of the hotels and wander down to the beach.

4 SENGGIGI

This series of sweeping bays has become Lombok's best-known stretch of coastline, and recently home to countless major hotel chains including a Sheraton. Further along the road, however, are several just as magnificent and unspoiled beaches fringed by palm trees and overlooked by steep cliffs.

From Senggigi, continue a further 20km through impressive scenery to Pemenang and then take the left turning to Bangsal.

5 BANGSAL

This little village marks the departure point for the three idyllic offshore islands of Gili Air, Gili Meno and Gili Trawangan. Charter a boat for a quick tour of the islands, or take one of the public boats and spend the night in relative tropical splendour.

From Bangsal, head back to the crossroads at Pemenang and continue straight on the road to Mataram. After 10km you will reach Baun Pusak, situated at the highest point of the road.

6 BAUN PUSAK

Set in magnificent scenery at the end of a stretch of road that climbs past rice fields and lush trees inhabited by monkeys, this mountain pass offers one of the finest panoramas in the whole of Lombok. Climb up the steps next to the coffee shop from where, on a clear day, you can see the coastline and, occasionally, even the distant Gili Islands.

From Baun Pusak continue south for 13km along another fine stretch of road. At the main crossroads turn left for Mataram or continue for 2km to Ampenan.

THE SASAK PEOPLE

Small, dark skinned and clad in sarongs made of beautiful cloth, the Sasaks inhabit some 270 towns and villages throughout the island of Lombok. Like the Balinese, they are mainly farmers, but they also have their own mosques and their own set of rituals.

These days many of the inhabitants produce textiles for the burgeoning tourist industry; others have moved into the larger towns. You can still see glimpses of the old way of life, however, in the beautiful village of Sade and the nearby weaving community of Sukarara.

Left: working the fields
Below: Sasak woman at Kuta Beach market day

Outwardly these people are more reserved than the Balinese. They wear different clothes, drink rice wine and practise weaving. Traditionally, too, the houses are distinct, built square or rectangular from bamboo and wood.

According to the most recent census, Lombok's Sasaks make up some 80 per cent of the island's 2.5 million population. They are also Lombok's original inhabitants, practising a form of Islam that is based on animism and ancestor worship.

GETTING AWAY FROM IT ALL

'Life is so simple and
primitive in the warmth of the
tropics. A bunch of bananas,
a basket of steamed
rice, and a leaf full of
betel comprise the
necessaries and
luxuries of daily
living.'

**E.R.
SCIDMORE,**
*Java, The Garden
of the East* (1899)

INTRODUCTION

Java, Bali and Lombok offer some wonderful places to escape to, and there are plenty of opportunities to explore islands further afield as well. Many of the trips can be done with minimal planning, others demand a little more time and effort but can be equally rewarding. Before deciding what you want to do, check on weather conditions and availability of transport. If in doubt seek advice from the tourist office in Jakarta (tel: (021) 310 3117) or Denpasar (tel: (0361) 223 87).

MOUNTAINS AND VOLCANOES

Indonesia has mountains and volcanoes to suit every taste, from gentle inclines to erupting giants. To check on conditions, always consult the locals before you go. Be sure to take warm clothes and on the tougher approaches a guide as well. Finally, if it is clear views that you are after, it is imperative to get to the summit at dawn, which means climbing at night with the use of torches.

Gunung Agung

This giant peak, soaring 3,142m high, is the tallest mountain on Bali and offers fantastic views. You will have to be fit to get to the top though as the tough 5-hour hike involves a series of steep paths, slippery slopes and narrow ridges. Make sure you take a guide as paths lead off in all directions, plus a thick sweater, food, water and bags of enthusiasm.
Location: approach from Pura Besakih, 60km northeast of Denpasar. Bemos operate via KlungKung (22km). Simple accommodation is available near the temple. Enquire locally for guides.

Gunung Batur

Towering over beautiful Lake Batur is Bali's fourth highest mountain and one of the most spectacular points from which to view sunrise. You can climb it in 2 hours with good shoes (take a torch if you attempt it at night), and ideally a guide who will take along breakfast. By setting off at around 3am from the village of Kedisan you should be at the top well before dawn. For information or guides, enquire at the local guesthouses.
Location: 4km east of Penelokan, near the village of Kedisan. Regular buses run from Denpasar and Kuta. Accommodation is available.

Gunung Bromo (Mount Bromo), see pages 72–3.

Gunung Merapi

Meteorologists claim that this is one of Java's most formidable volcanoes, erupting on average once every six years. Mount Merapi is also one of Java's most rewarding, if difficult, climbs taking 4 or 5 hours to get to the summit and a further 3 hours to descend. For the easier approach, start from Selo just to the north of Merapi where guides are available. Take plenty of warm clothes and a torch. It is also possible to climb from Kaliurang, although this is a considerably tougher route taking a minimum of 6 hours to reach the summit.
Location: Selo lies 50km west of Surakarta (Solo), in Central Java. Buses leave for Kartusuro from the Umbunharjo bus station off Jalan Veteran. Change again for Boyolali and catch a bemo to Selo. Accommodation is available at Selo.

Gunung Rinjani

Dominating the whole of Lombok, this magnificent 3,726m mountain is the

To enjoy clear views of the mountains you must climb at dawn

second highest in Indonesia outside Irian Jaya. To climb it, you will need at least 2 days and considerable amounts of energy. Best to start in the town of Bayan, ascending via Senaru and returning the same way. Although there are now plenty of travellers doing the trip alone, you are strongly advised to take a local guide who can organise food and sleeping bags. For alternative and more testing routes, enquire locally.

Location: northern Lombok. Bemos leave from Cakranegara's Sweta terminal for Bayan, where you have to catch another bemo to Senaru. Basic accommodation is available at Senaru.

Distinguished sea-faring vessels in the port of Sulawesi

ISLAND HOPPING

To explore some of the dazzling islands that make up the Indonesian archipelago all you need is a handful of money, a grand sense of humour and lots of time. Boats leave from literally hundreds of ports, making their way by river and by sea to some of the least visited parts of the country.

Note, however, that schedules change from day to day and month to month, the only certainty being that boats leave when you least expect them to. The best season for island hopping is between May and October. During the rainy season it can be wet and rough, and extremely unpleasant.

For details about the national shipping line on Java, contact Pelni, Jalan Angkasa Kemayoran 18, Jakarta (tel: 421 7406).

For Bali, contact the Pelni office on Jalan Pelabuhan Benoa, Denpasar (tel: 28962). For Lombok, contact the Pelni office at Jalan Industri 1, Ampenan (tel: 21604).

Sailing to Sumatra

Most passengers wishing to cross from Jakarta to Sumatra simply take a flight from Soekarno-Hatta Airport. Those looking for a more enjoyable alternative, however, can take the weekly Pelni ship from Jakarta's port of Tanjung Priok to Padang (and back). It's a relatively luxurious boat, with hot water and a restaurant, and you should make a reservation before departure. Tickets can be bought at Pelni's Jakarta office: Jalan Angkasa Kemayoran 18 (tel: 421 7406).

Visitors preferring a cheaper and

more authentic means of transport can take a boat from the island of Tanjung Pinang (off the coast of Singapore) to Pekanbaru in Central Sumatra. Generally it leaves three or four times a week, is typically crowded, hot, and when it rains, wet. Take food and reckon on a 36-hour journey, although as with everything in Sumatra, prepare for the exception.

Island Chain

Beyond Bali, Java and Lombok lie countless other islands, many of them less than an hour away by air, others a few days by cargo boat. Some offer jungles, others uninhabited mountains, strange tribes and beautiful coloured lakes. Many are so small that they are not even named.

A Pelni passenger boat leaves every 2 weeks or so from Surabaya in East Java to the port of Lembar on Lombok and from there to Ujung Pandang (Sulawesi), Bima (Sumbawa), Wainngapu (Sumba) and Ende (Flores). Other passenger or cargo boats depart with far greater regularity between Lombok and the outer islands. For a real taste of adventure drop by the old port of Sunda Kelapa in Jakarta and try and get a passage on one of the old Bugis schooners that still occasionally make the voyage to the islands of Flores and Timor. You may have to sleep on the deck or work your passage, but you are likely to have a memorable experience.

Five-star Cruising

Looking for a cruise without any hassle? These days there are plenty of opportunities, with good food, white wine and even hot showers. On Bali, for a short trip, take the Bali Hai Cruise

aboard a fully air-conditioned 34m luxury catamaran that accommodates 300 passengers and visits the islands of Nusa Penida or Nusa Lembongan. Day trips as well as sunset cruises are offered leaving from Benoa Harbour, Bali Hai Pier (tel: (361) 34331).

P&0 Spice Island Cruises also offer an island-hopping expedition, but for an 8-day/7-night programme. The route goes east from Bali to Lombok, Sumbawa, Komodo Island and Flores. For details contact: P & O Spice Island Cruises, Jalan Jen Parmen 78, Jakarta Barat (tel: (021) 593 401/2).

Slow boats off the Java coast, in Baluran National Park

FLORA AND FAUNA

At dusk, the sweet smell of frangipani mingles with the scented odours of Jepun trees and hibiscus. Great boughs of bougainvillaea cascade in sheer tropical splendour alongside scented capoka and dozens of varieties of orchids dazzle the senses.

On Java, Bali and Lombok alone you will find over 5,000 species of plants, plus more than 500 types of birds, from the white-bellied sea eagle and the olive-backed sunbird to the small blue kingfisher, as well as the famous Rothschild's mynah, Bali's only endemic bird.

Despite massive deforestation and the rape of large areas of parkland, you can still spot a multitude of animals, from the long-tailed macaques to wild pigs and silvered leaf monkeys. Even leopards have been reported on the crowded island of Java, although these days sightings are exceptionally rare.

The best places to experience nature at its most beautiful are in the Javanese national parks of Ujung Kulon and Baluran, or at the Bali Barat

Left: rainforest, Java
Far left (main):
Baluran National
Park
Far left (inset): lotus
flowers
Below: wild flowers,
Lombok
Bottom: East Java

National Park. But wander away from the towns, the cities and the endless rice fields and you will catch a glimpse not necessarily of tigers, but of brightly coloured flowers and lush countryside – remnants of one of the earth's greatest tropical paradises.

NATIONAL PARKS

Nestling amid the hills and forests of Java and Bali lie a handful of fine national parks, although you may have to travel a considerable distance to get to them. Some are renowned as the homes of the few remaining Javanese rhinoceros, others are simply pleasant places to walk in. Before leaving Jakarta, contact the PHPA office on Jalan Merdeka Selatan 8–9 Blok G to enquire about permits and accommodation. Bring binoculars if you have them and a lot of patience. Note that in the wet season some of the parks may be inaccessible.

Baluran Taman Nasional

One of the greatest attractions of the Baluran National Park is its relative accessibility. The park lies just 37km from Ketapang, the main crossing point from Java to Bali, covering an area of 250 sq km and dominated by Mount Baluran. Although large areas of the park are arid and savannah-like, at dusk especially you can see herds of deer, wild pig and buffalo. Bring food if you intend to stay overnight and sign in at the main visitors' centre (see page 72).

Meru Betiri Taman Nasional

The Meru Betiri Reserve lies at the end of a potholed road that crosses half a dozen rivers, and forest and rubber plantations. Until the 1940s, this was a popular area for spotting the small Javanese tiger. These days, if you are lucky, you may come across black

Large tracts of forest and savannah are found at Baluran Taman Nasional

panthers, leopards and even turtles. There is basic accommodation in Sukamade village (Turtle Beach) or contact the PHPA Guesthouse at Rajegwesin village.

Location: 70km west of Genteng in East Java. Buses leave from the Banjarsari terminal in Banyuwangi for Genteng, where you have to take an irregular bus or hitch a lift to Sukamade.

Pulau Dua Bird Sanctuary

Ornithologists will have a field day in this sanctuary on Dua Island, which lies in Banten Bay off the coast of West Java. One of Indonesia's best-known bird parks, Pulau Dua boasts more than 50 species of bird including ibises and egrets. Get there between April and August to see it at its liveliest, and take food and water.

Location: 100km west of Jakarta. Buses depart from Jakarta's Kalideres station for Serang, from where you must catch a bemo to Banten. From the Karanghantu harbour in Banten, it is a half-hour boat ride. Currently there is a guesthouse, but no restaurant.

Taman Nasional Bali Barat (Bali Barat National Park)

Once upon a time visitors would have come across tigers in this sparsely populated region of Bali. These days the animals you are most likely to see in the 200 sq km of coastal forest are long-tailed macaques, barking and sambar deer, or, if you are really lucky, the Rothschild's mynah, which is Bali's only endemic bird. Several trails start out from Labuhan Lalang, 15km from the visitors' centre. Alternatively, take the delightful boat trip to Menjangan Island, a 30-minute trip from the mainland. To arrange a guide and accommodation go

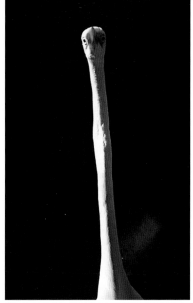

The opportunity of seeing rare bird species like the egret is the real attraction of Pulau Dua

to the visitors' centre, which is situated on the main road 3km from Gilimanuk.

Location: 134km northwest of Denpasar. Buses leave from Denpasar's Ubung terminal for Gilimanuk, taking 3 to 4 hours. Ask to be dropped off at the park headquarters.

Ujung Kulon Taman Nasional

Lying in the westernmost corner of Java, hemmed in by the Indian Ocean, this magnificent national park boasts several of the rare Javanese rhinoceros as well as leopards, gibbons, long-tailed macaques and herds of oxen. To get there, you can either catch a boat from Labuhan to Peucang island, which takes 5 or 6 hours, or arrange a tour. Make reservations and obtain a permit at the PHPA office on Jalan Perintis Kemerdekaan 43 in Labuhan.

Location: Labuhan is situated 120km west of Jakarta. Buses leave Jakarta's Kalideres station. Boats leave from Labuhan for Peucang Island twice weekly.

Collecting firewood in Java's central hills

HILL STATIONS

When the Dutch occupied Indonesia they not only constructed fine buildings and grand open squares, but also charming mountain retreats so they could escape the heat of the tropics. Many of these resorts offer unsurpassed views of distant volcanoes; others hot springs where you can rest your weary limbs. If you visit the hill resorts at weekends rooms may be hard to come by and the places inundated by crowds. At other times you may find yourself almost alone, but for the trees and bubbling streams.

Kaliurang

This pretty little resort, 900m up on Merapi's southern slope, is a fine weekday getaway with waterfalls, swimming pools and cool mountain air.

If you are here during the dry season, get up early to catch the spectacular sunrise and clear views of Mount Merapi. More active visitors can climb to Merapi's summit, although for your own safety you are advised to take a guide (see page 59).

Location: 24km north of Yogyakarta in Central Java. Regular buses leave from the main Umbulharjo terminal on Jalan Kemerdekan, taking 90 minutes.

Sarangan

This little town lies at the end of one of the most spectacular stretches of road on the whole of Java. Here, on the panoramic slopes of Mount Lawu, visitors can explore the crater and nearby waterfall, go speed-boating on the small lake as well as fishing and horse-back riding on fine-bred horses.

Not surprisingly, the Dutch took a liking to the place and built mountain villas commanding fine views of the area. If you come at weekends, be sure to have reserved a room. At other times of the year it's a perfect place to soothe nerves frayed by days of sightseeing in Solo and Yogyakarta.

Location: 55km east of Surakarta (Solo) in Central Java. Buses run from the Tirtonadi terminal on Jalan Jend Yani to Tawangmangu, from where you can catch a crowded bemo *for the last 30-minute stretch.*

Selekta

You will find all the pine trees and bubbling streams that you can dream of above this up-market hill resort, along with orchards, strawberries and fine mountain scenery. In the centre of town there is a recreational centre, built by the Dutch and containing a delightful rock garden and swimming pool.

Location: 23km from Malang in East Java. Buses leave from Malang's central bus station on Jalan Haryono. Alternatively, rent a taxi.

Tawangmangu

Dutch villas and simple *losmen* (bungalows) dot the hills around Tawangmangu, on the slopes of Gunug Lawu, which offers fine walks and mountain scenery. As a pleasant side trip, visit Sarangan (14km), or head west to the famous 15th-century Candi Sukuh, built during the Majapahit empire then mysteriously abandoned.

Location: 42km from Solo in Central Java. Buses leave from the Tirtonadi station on Jalan Jend Yani, taking 90 minutes.

The lush, tropical foliage around Jekut Waterfalls, near beautiful Tetebatu

Tetebatu

Surrounded by rice fields and offering magnificent views of Mount Rinjani, this is Lombok's most popular inland retreat. There are walks to a nearby waterfall, paddies where you can wander for days, as well as cooler mountain air (see page 129).

Tretes

This town in East Java is renowned for its popular hill resort and for its brothels. Nature lovers follow hiking trails around Mount Arjuna and Mount Welirang, visit waterfalls or go horse riding and swimming. Those in search of other activities can enjoy a no less varied menu.

Location: 55km south of Surabaya. Take the bus heading for Malang and ask to be dropped off at Pandakan. From here you can catch a bemo *to Tretes.*

OTHER ACTIVITIES

Birdwatching

Javanese kingfishers, blue-tailed bee-eaters, Sunda minnivets and white-breasted woodswallows are just some of the birds that can be seen on Java, Bali and Lombok, so long as you have the time and the patience. Good places to spot them include the Pula Dua Bird Sanctuary near Banten in West Java (see page 141), the Bali Barat National Park in western Bali (see page 141), the Baluran National Park in East Java (see page 140) and the steep cliffs on the island of Nusa Penida (see page 88). For those wanting to observe birds the easy way, visit the Taman Burung (Bird Park) at Taman Mini Indonesia in east Jakarta (see page 39) or the Ragunan Zoo in south Jakarta (see pages 32–3).

Cycling

Taking a bicycle around Java, Bali or Lombok may be hot, hard work, but it is a good way to see the countryside. Bicycles can now be hired in Kuta, Ubud and from many small *losmen* and guesthouses throughout the country.

Diving

There are plenty of opportunities for diving in Indonesia, ranging from Pulau Seribu (Thousand Islands, see page 48) a short distance from Jakarta, to Pulau Menjangan in the Bali Barat National Park (see page 141) and the increasingly popular Gili Islands on Lombok (see page 124). Keen divers also head for Balina Beach (see page 84) and Tulamben on Bali (see page 91), where you can rent gear. For enquiries, contact Oceana Dive Centre, Sanur Beach (tel: 88652) which organises diving vacations.

Motorbiking

Although motorbiking is not popular on Java, on Bali almost everyone seems to use one. Bikes are generally 75cc and can be rented from anywhere in Kuta, Denpasar or Ubud. Most visitors tour the island from Kuta, and you can take a motorbike over to Lombok on the ferry. Wherever you go, however, remember to lock the bike securely, obtain insurance and, most importantly, drive carefully as accidents are common.

Diving off Benoa

DIRECTORY

> *The dominating fact about the islands is that, like Croesus and John D. Rockefeller, Jr., they are rich. They are the Big Loot of Asia.*
> **JOHN GUNTHER,**
> *Inside Asia*
> (1939)

Shopping

*F*rom beautiful wooden carvings to colourful batik and the eye-catching Wayang Kulit shadow puppets, Indonesia offers a bewildering choice of shopping opportunities. You can stock up on hand-woven textiles, musical instruments or even vast demonic stone carvings – although you may have trouble transporting these home.

On Bali, and especially around the village of Ubud, there is a wealth of artistic talent and this is reflected in the paintings, sculptures and silverwork on sale. On Lombok, beautiful terracotta jars made by the Sasaks can be found all over the island, as well as woven baskets. Indeed, the only thing that is both expensive and in short supply in Indonesia is electronic goods, so if that is what you are after, arrange a stop-over in neighbouring Singapore.

A Way of Life

Going shopping in Indonesia is not so much a necessity as a source of enjoyment. Prices can be as flexible as the attitude of the buyer and time an irrelevant commodity.

To see that attitude at its most prevalent you must visit the markets, but even in the shops and boutiques, where prices tend to be fixed, you will find a charm and helpfulness that is hard to come by in most European countries.

Don't buy the first thing that you set your eyes on though. A better approach is to spend a few days looking around to get an idea of what is on offer. That way you will avoid amassing too many second-rate tourist articles and should be better equipped to negotiate good prices.

Value for Money

For cheap and cheerful items, but often of inferior quality, drop by the markets in the major towns. Next up the scale are the small studios and art galleries specialising in batik, woodcarvings or paintings. In Ubud and in Yogyakarta especially these studios provide greater choice and lower prices as they do not employ middlemen.

For comfort, take your pick of the modern shopping plazas that now abound in the big cities, especially in

Bird cages for sale in Pasar Ngasem, Yogyakarta

Sunday market in Kuta, on the island of Lombok

Jakarta. At Sarinah Department Store, on Jalan Thamrin, there is one of the widest choices of handicrafts in the whole country. Finally, at the top of the scale, are the larger hotels which sell arts and crafts from all over Indonesia.

As a rule, no matter where you are, always try to bargain by offering a considerably lower price than is advertised. At worst you will get a look of bemusement, at best a considerable discount. One last piece of advice: beware the ubiquitous touts, who will offer to take you shopping free of charge. They may not be getting money out of you directly, but they will certainly be paid a 10–20 per cent commission, which will be added on to the articles you buy.

MARKETS

Street markets can be found in towns and villages throughout Java, Bali and Lombok, selling everything from exotic fruits to water taps and from ancient magazines to fake Levi jeans. In some markets you can feast yourself on deep-fried dragonfly, stuffed duck or even pigs' balls. In others you will see beautiful woven baskets, sweet-smelling flowers or carved wooden monkeys. For antiques and imitation trinkets, Pasar Triwindu in Surakarta (see page 69), or Jalan Surabaya in Jakarta (see page 33) are worth a browse. For something more flighty, ask for the Pasar Ngasem, or bird market, in Yogyakarta (see page 54). Wherever you go you will find a rich tapestry of life second to none; take a camera and lots of film, you won't be disappointed. To find a market simply ask for *pasar*, and for the night market, *pasar malam*.

WHAT TO BUY

ANTIQUES

Renowned for its delightful antique masks, its *krises* (ceremonial daggers), and much prized betel nut sets, Indonesia is acquiring an even bigger reputation for its fakes. Unless you are a real expert or are content to buy an imitation, take the claims of any shop owner with a pinch of salt, especially in Jakarta's antique market on Jalan Surabaya, and concentrate on buying some more worthy article.

BRONZE AND BRASS CASTING

Bronze bells, musical instruments and cast statues are a speciality of the little town of Klungkung on Bali, but there are plenty of similar articles available in all the main cities on Java. Big tourist shops will have the widest choice of items and for a price they will be able to arrange shipment of the articles back to Europe.

CERAMICS AND PORCELAIN

Since the art was introduced from China more than 700 years ago, potters have been turning out fine ceramics and porcelain in Indonesia ever since. You'll find the most beautiful terracotta pots on Lombok and it is worth keeping an eye out for old Han dynasty pottery, T'ang ceramics and even choice Ming period porcelain.

PAINTINGS

Paintings on Bali are almost as abundant as rice fields, especially in the area around Ubud which has become the cultural capital of the island. You will

Local handmade baskets in Kuta village, Lombok

find plenty of the soporific village scenes, cock-fights and festivals that are churned out for undemanding tourists, but also some of the country's finest paintings that combine the traditional Balinese style with the influence of foreign artists like Walter Spies and Rudolf Bonnet. To get an idea of the quality, check out the Museum Neka in Ubud (see page 110) and when shopping for paintings, remember to be extremely selective.

SILVERWORK

If Ubud's *pièce de résistance* is its paintings, then Celuk's reputation is based on its silverwork (see page 101). Artisans in this little village run up bracelets, pendants and rings – all at relatively low prices. Elsewhere on Bali, and even Java, you'll find plenty of other ornate pieces, often decorated with filigree.

STONE CARVINGS

Most people take one look at the monstrous weight of these stone figures and move on to something more manageable. But these days, the more commercially minded masons will arrange to have them shipped anywhere in the world. To see what's on offer, check out the village of Batubulan (see page 100) on Bali. Here you can watch the artists at work and even order your own tailor-made stone demon.

TEXTILES

One of the finest of all Indonesia's arts, batik, which is cloth painted and dyed with bright colours, makes the perfect gift. The best places for batik include Yogyakarta and Surakarta in Central Java, as well as Ubud on Bali, but almost everywhere you will find beautiful silks and colourful sarongs – and occasionally even double Ikat, the finely woven and

To purchase the best stone carvings visit Batubulan on Bali

dyed cloth made in several Bali Aga villages.

WOODCARVINGS

Spectacular woodcarvings are a Balinese speciality, and nowhere more so than around Ubud and in the village of Mas (see page 114). Collectors' items range from teak fruit bowls to sandalwood statuettes and magnificent Garuda birds. There's no shortage of hideous wooden elephants and cheap, lurid carvings either, so be selective and shop around.

WOVEN GOODS

If a woven basket made from rattan is what you are after, then Lombok is the place to go, with a variety and price second to none. There are plenty of similar articles on Bali too, although at higher prices.

Jalan Surabaya, Jakarta

WHERE TO BUY

Wherever you go in Indonesia you will find beautiful hand-made items, carved wooden statues or pearl-studded bracelets. However, remember to be selective and bargain hard.

Below is a list of popular shops in the main centres. If these look expensive, simply check out others in the vicinity.

JAKARTA
Antiques
Djap Art Shop, *Plaza Indonesia, Shop No 49–50, Basement 1, Jalan Thamrin (tel: 332 191).*
Gedung Kesenian Galleries, *Jalan Gedung Kesenian 1, Pasar Baru (tel: 750 2827).*
Johan Art Curio, *Jalan Salim 59A (tel: 336 023).*
Rama Art Curio & Antiques, *Jalan Kebon Sirih Timur Dalem 21 (tel: 325 983).*
Tribal, *Hotel Borobudur, Jalan Lapangan Banteng Selatan (tel: 380 5555).*

Handicrafts
Artshop, *Jalan Pasar Baru 15 (tel: 360 524).*
Hadi Handicraft, *Plaza Indonesia, Jalan Thamrin, 144–145, Level 1 (tel: 310 7574).*

Irian Art & Gift Shop, *Jalan Pasar Baru 16 (tel: 343 422).*
Jakarta Handicrafts Centre, *Jalan Pekalongan 12A (tel: 338 157).*
Keris Gallery, *Jalan Cokroaminoto 87–89 (tel: 334 516).*

Jewellery and Silverware
Dynasty Collection, *Ratu Plaza, Jalan Sudirman (tel: 711 815).*
Indonesian Opal and Jewellery Centre, *Plaza Indonesia, Shop No 112, Level 1, Jalan Thamrin (tel: 327 866).*
Silverthreads, *Plaza Indonesia, Shop No 143, Level 1, Jalan Thamrin (tel: 333 362).*

Silk, Cotton and Batik
Batik Mira, *Jalan Raya 22 (tel: 761 138).*
Batik Shani, *Plaza Indonesia, Shop No 120, Level 1, Jalan Thamrin (tel: 326 620).*
Djody Art & Curio, *Jalan Kebon Sirih Timur Dalem A22 (tel: 347 730).*
GKBI, *Indonesian Government Batik Co-operative, Jalan Sudirman 28 (tel: 581 022).*

Shopping Centres
Plaza Indonesia, *Jalan Thamrin Kav 28–30 (tel: 3107 272).*
Sarinah Department Store, *Jalan Thamrin No 11 (tel: 327 425).*

Woodcarvings
Ida Bagus Tilem Gallery, *Mandarin Oriental Jakarta Hotel Shopping Arcade, Jalan Thamrin (tel: 321 1307).*

YOGYAKARTA
Antiques
Ancient Arts, *Jalan Tirtodipuran 30.*

Ardijanto's, *Jalan Magelag, Km 5.8 (tel: 87777)*.
Kerajinan Indonesia, *Jalan Marlboro 193–195 (tel: 87995)*.

Batik and Cotton
Batik Keris, *Jalan Ahmad Yani 104 (tel: 2492)*.
Batik Griya Timur, *Jalan Ahmad Yani 25 (tel: 2844)*.
Batik Gurda, *Jalan Parangtritis 77 (tel: 5474)*.
Batik Plentong, *Jalan Tirtodipuran 28 (tel: 2777)*.
Toko Terang Bulan, *Jalan Ahmad Yani 76 (tel: 2488)*.

Handicrafts
Art Shop Naga, *Jalan Malioboro 61*.
Mirota Batik, *Jalan Ahmad Yani 9 (tel: 4620)*.
Moeljosoehardjo's, *Jalan Taman Sari 37B (tel: 2873)*.
Yogyakarta Craft Centre,
Jalan Laksda Adisucipto (tel: 4526).

Silver and Jewellery
M D Silver, *Jalan Keboan, Kota Gede (tel: 2063)*.
Moeljo's Silver, *Jalan Menteri Supeno UH XII/1 (tel: 88042)*.
Tjokrosoeharto, *Jalan Panembahan 58 (tel: 3208)*.
Tom's Silver, *Jalan Ngeksiganda, Kota Gede (tel: 3070)*.

DENPASAR
Art Shops
Besakih Artshop, *Jalan Surapati 20 (tel: 22879)*.
Handayana House of Arts, *Jalan Gianyar (tel: 2662)*.
Mega Gallery of Arts, *Jalan Raya Gianyar, Tohpati (tel: 28855)*.

Intricate textile design, Yogyakarta

Pelangi Artshop, *Jalan Gajah Mada 44 (tel: 24570)*.

Handicrafts
Kumbasari Artmarket, *Jalan Gajah Mada*.
Sanggraha Kriya Asta, *Tohpati (tel: 22942)*.
Sri Ratih, *Jalan Gajah Mada, 36 (tel: 24592)*.
Yudistira, *Jalan Gajah Mada 42 (tel: 22712)*.

Popular batik, Yogyakarta

Entertainment

You need never be bored on Java or Bali. Whether it's nightclubs in Jakarta or Sanur, shadow puppets in Yogyakarta, or Legong dances in Ubud, there is enough on offer to keep everybody happy. Many discothèques stay open until the early hours of the morning and even traditional entertainment like the Wayang Kulit shadow puppets can last until late at night. For something a little different, there are night markets, *gamelan* orchestras and sometimes illegal cock-fights. Most hotels will provide information on local events; or refer to the entertainment section of the local papers.

BARS

Visitors expecting to find an equivalent to neighbouring Bangkok's nightlife may not be entirely disappointed. While Indonesia does not have the go-go bars of Thailand, it does have the drinking establishments and massage parlours. Most of these are to be found in Jakarta's China Town, although Yogyakarta and even Surabaya can boast more than a handful, and on Bali's Kuta Beach you will find almost as many bars as there are on the rest of the archipelago put together. Only on Lombok is the bar scene almost non-existent, except for those in the big luxurious hotels at Senggigi Beach and among the plethora of little guesthouses on Kuta Beach and the Gili Islands.

For drama and violence Indonesian films are in a class of their own

Jakarta is the home to a mind-boggling range of nightclubs

CINEMAS

Cinemas abound in Jakarta and in all the major towns, although generally they show local films with no English subtitles. Any Western films that do make it tend to be heavily censored. For details of programmes, check the local newspaper or ask in your hotel. Also, while in Jakarta, check out the British Council, Jalan Jend Sudirman 57 (tel: 587 4411) and the Alliance Française, Jalan Salemba Rayes 25, both of which schedule weekly films.

COCKTAIL LOUNGES

All the luxury hotels have cocktail lounges where you can while away the time by a pool-side terrace or in a lush garden setting. Many hotels even host jazz bands or local musicians. For a glimpse of the real Java or Bali, however, you must leave these classy establishments, wander along the beaches or down the main streets and explore some of the places frequented by the local people. These will not only be cheaper, but they will give you a feel of what the real Indonesia is all about.

DISCOTHEQUES AND LIVE MUSIC

People may dismiss Indonesia as a musical backwater, but Jakarta and the major resort areas not only have some of the biggest and most modern dance floors in the developing world, but some of the trendiest people on them. There is now a Hard Rock Café in Jakarta, countless discos, as well as several excellent venues for local bands. Elsewhere, new and exciting nightclubs are springing up every month. Entry to nightclubs is relatively cheap by Western standards, with a free drink often thrown in with the price. Expect to pay more at weekends.

KARAOKE LOUNGES

Although relatively new, karaoke lounges in Jakarta are already becoming big business. If singing along to a video is your idea of fun, there are plenty of places to choose from. Outside the major towns, however, karaoke is likely to mean little more than music in a massage parlour.

WHERE TO GO

JAKARTA
Cultural Performances
Bharata Theatre
Traditional *wayang orang* dance drama performed nightly, except Saturday, between 8pm and 11pm.
Jalan Pasar Senen 15.
Hotel Borobudur
Friday evening buffet and cultural show beginning at 7pm.
Jalan Lapangan Banteng Selatan (tel: 380 5555).
Taman Ismail Marzuki
Regular cultural shows and performances. Check newspaper for details.
Jalan Cikini Raya 73, Menteng (tel: 322 606).
Taman Mini-Indonesia
Sunday performances of drama, dance and music, taking place between 9am and 2pm.
10km southeast of Jakarta (see page 39).
Wayang Museum
Displays of shadow puppets twice monthly on Sundays at 10am. Telephone for details.
Jalan Pintu Besar Utara (tel: 679 560).

Discos
Fire Disco, *Plaza Indonesia, Jalan Thamrin.*
Music Room, *Borobudur Intercontinental, Jalan Lapangan Banteng Selatan (tel: 380 5555).*
Oriental Club, *Hilton Hotel, Jalan Gatot Subroto (tel: 570 3600).*
Pitstop, *Sari Pan Pacific Hotel, Jalan Thamrin 6 (tel: 323 707).*
Stardust, *Jayakarta Tower Hotel, Jalan Hayam Wuruk (tel: 629 4408).*
Tanamur, *Jalan Abang Timur 14 (tel: 353 947).*

Pubs
Green Pub
Live music combined with Mexican food.
Djakarta Theatre Building, Jalan Thamrin (tel: 359 332).
Hard Rock Café
Popular western bar/restaurant.
Jalan Thamrin.
Jaya Pub
Live music and pub food.
Jaya Building, Jalan Thamrin No 12 (tel: 325 633).
Melati Lounge
Western and local jazz.
Sari Pan Pacific Hotel, Jalan Thamrin 6 (tel: 323 707).
O'Reiley's Pub
Top-class hotel pub with beer on tap and band.
Grand Hyatt Jakarta, Jalan Thamrin 28–30 (tel: 310 7400).
Pete's Tavern
Live music and pub food.
Argo Pantes Building, Jalan Gatot Subroto (tel 515 478).

Shows
International Hailai Club
Las Vegas-style floor show, dance troupes, restaurant and disco.
Hailai Building, Jalan Lodan, Ancol (tel: 689 868).
Taman Ismail Marzuki
Cultural and performing arts centre of Jakarta.
Jalan Cikini Raya 73, Menteng (tel: 322 606).

YOGYAKARTA
Cultural Performances
Agastya Art Institute
Wayang Kulit performance, Sunday to Friday.
Jalan Gedongkiwo.

Ambarbudaya Craft Centre
Open: Monday, Wednesday and
Saturday, 9.30pm–10.30pm.
Jalan Adisucipto.
Ambarrukmo Palace Hotel
Performances of the Ramayana, Monday,
Wednesday and Saturday, 8pm.
Jalan Adisucipto (tel: 88488).
Arjuna Plaza Hotel (French Grill)
Wayang Kulit performance on Tuesday,
7pm–9pm.
Jalan Mangkubumi 48 (tel: 86862).
Dalem Pujokusuman
Performances of the *Ramayana*,
Monday, Wednesday and Friday,
8pm–10pm.
Jalan Katamso.
Kraton Yogyakarta
Gamelan rehearsals at 10.30am–noon on
Monday and Wednesday mornings.
Alun Alun (tel: 2889).
Prambanan Royal Ballet
Open-air performances held at
Prambanan between May to October on
the nights of the full moon.
Tel: (0274) 96408 for details.
Sono Budoyo Museum
Wayang Kulit performances held every
night (except Monday), 8pm–10pm.
*Northwest side of Alun-Alun Lor (tel:
2775).*
THR Amusement Park
Nightly performances of wayang orang at
8pm.
Jalan Brig Jen Katamso.

KUTA
Discos
Spotlight
Vast dance floor, pounding music and
western travellers.
Jalan Legian.
Chez Gado-Gado
Up-market beachfront night-club.
Dyana Pura Lane, north of Legian.

A temple celebration, Bali

Peanuts
Popular pub/disco.
Jalan Legian.

SANUR
Classical Dance
Buffet dinner and classical dance,
Monday and Wednesday.
Sanur Beach Hotel (tel: 88011).
Tanjung Sari Hotel
Jalan Tanjung Sari (tel: 88441).

Discos
Matahari Disco
Small and relatively exclusive.
*Bali Hyatt Hotel, Jalan Tanjung Sari (tel:
88271).*
Number One
Up-market place with no shorts, thongs
or singlets allowed.
*Jalan Tanjung Sari, at the southern end of
Sanur (tel: 8097).*
Subec
Funky light systems and big crowds.
Jalan Tanjung Sari.

UBUD
Cultural Performances
Puri Saren Palace
Performances of the Ramayana, Legong,
Barong and Kecak held most nights of the
week. Enquire locally for details.
*Jalan Raya (next to the junction with
Monkey Forest Road).*

BALINESE FESTIVALS

The first light of dawn sees the locals already hard at work in the little bamboo huts that cluster around Lake Bratan, preparing their offerings of oil and betel nut, putting on their finest silks or simply placing gifts of rice and joss sticks on the ground for the local spirits.

Some of the men will have been up for hours, roasting the suckling pigs and ducks over a fire then placing them on banana leaves.

By 10am the first groups of women leave for the temple, carrying magnificent piles of fruit and other delicacies on trays above their heads. Inside the inner courtyard the offerings are blessed by the priests, sprinkled with holy water and offered up as food for the gods.

The *odalan* festival is not unique to this tiny village. Throughout Bali, similar festivals are held for a temple birthday, for a Hindu holiday, or simply to give thanks to the gods for creating this earthly paradise.

Around the Balinese new year especially, countless ceremonies take place to celebrate the cleansing of the evil spirits or to honour the goddess of knowledge or the victory of virtue over evil. Some villages have temple ceremonies as thanks for the local rice crop, others to maintain equilibrium between the forces of good and evil.

Ceremonies are also held to celebrate each stage of a child's life from conception to birth through to death and the joyous release of the spirit.

Whatever the ceremony, you will almost inevitably see great processions

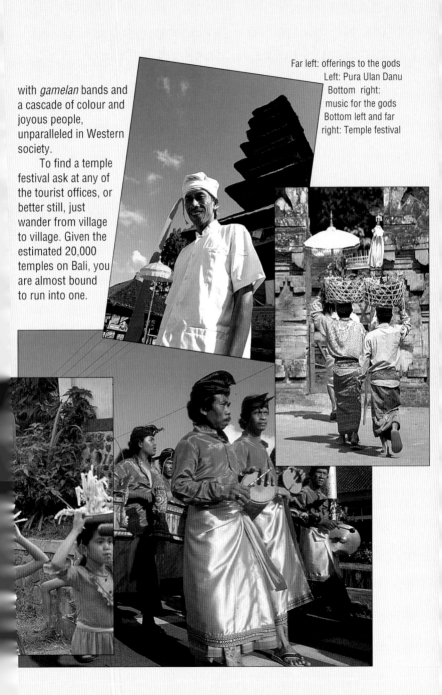

with *gamelan* bands and a cascade of colour and joyous people, unparalleled in Western society.

To find a temple festival ask at any of the tourist offices, or better still, just wander from village to village. Given the estimated 20,000 temples on Bali, you are almost bound to run into one.

Far left: offerings to the gods
Left: Pura Ulan Danu
Bottom right:
music for the gods
Bottom left and far
right: Temple festival

TRADITIONAL FORMS OF ENTERTAINMENT

Although disco dancing may be all the rage in the big cities, in the smaller towns and villages there are plenty of traditional forms of entertainment – just keep your eyes open and follow the crowds. Details of the larger, most popular events can be obtained from the local tourist authorities.

CLASSICAL DANCES

The most supremely elegant spectacle in Indonesia is not so much a form of entertainment as a work of art. Balinese girls as young as 3 learn the elaborate hand gestures and carefully prescribed movements of the Legong dance, and by the age of 11 or 12 they are said to be too old to perform. Nor are the dances purely traditional. These days there are bumblebee dances, masked dances and frog dances to add to the vintage Barong and Ramayana. You'll find plenty of special dances laid on for tourists, but if you are lucky you may find the real thing being performed at a temple or during a local festival. For information about classical dances ask at your hotel or in any tourist office.

Barong

This popular dance recounts the tale of the virtuous lion-like Barong and his duel with Rangda, the wicked witch. It's filled with colour, with magical battles and even a touch of comedy. Although mainly shown on Bali, you may occasionally find displays put on in Jakarta.

Kecak

The sound of monkeys chattering replaces the *gamelan* orchestra in this modern dance which tells a story from the *Ramayana*. Extremely popular, it is performed by candlelight on Bali and ends with the rescue of Sita by an army of monkeys.

Legong

One of the most beautiful and stylised of all dances, the Legong is performed by girls as young as 8 or 9 wearing elaborate jewelled costumes. The story tells of the kidnapping of Princess Rangkesari by Prince Lasem and her final rejection of his impassioned pleas.

Ramayana

Taken from the popular Hindu epic, this great tale recounts the kidnapping of Sita, the wife of Rama, and her eventual rescue by Hanuman, King of the monkeys. Anyone who is in the vicinity of Prambanan during the months of May and October at full moon will have the chance to witness the most spectacular performance of all.

GAMELAN MUSIC

You will hear the gentle combination of flutes, gongs and kettledrums at weddings, funerals and dances all over Indonesia. The grandest, most elaborate *gamelan* orchestras are made up of as many as 80 instruments. Others are composed of a

Hanuman, king of the monkeys

Scenes from Bali's famous Legong (above) and Ramayana (above right) dances

handful of local musicians playing for the fun of it. *Gamelan* performances take place every Sunday morning in the Kraton in Yogyakarta and in the National Museum in Jakarta. Elsewhere, in restaurants, markets or even hotels, you may find yourself being serenaded.

Tourist dances

KECAK FIRE & TRANCE DANCE

EVERY:
• SUNDAY
• MONDAY
• WEDNESDAY
• FRIDAY

IN BONA VILLAGE
(12 KM. FROM UBUD)
TICKET RP 5000 (INCLUDE TRANSPORT)
LEAVE AT 6:00 PM. FROM HERE

WAYANG KULIT

The best place to see these boisterous, leather shadow puppets in action is either in Yogyakarta or in Surakarta, the traditional homes of the Wayang Kulit. But in Ubud, the cultural centre of Bali, in Jakarta and outside in the countryside too, keep your eyes open for one of Indonesia's favourite forms of entertainment.

LOCAL FESTIVITIES

While official Muslim holidays in Indonesia are fixed on the same date every year, many of the Hindu festivals on Bali depend on the position of the moon. To make sure you do not miss them, get hold of the list of local events issued by the tourist office. For details of national holidays, see the Practical Guide, page 185.

Children

*B*eautiful beaches, charming people and long sunny days means Indonesia can be the perfect holiday destination for children. Bali especially caters for the whole family, with a mind-boggling array of activities as well as paddling pools in many of the big hotels, and these days even child-minders can be found.

On Java and Lombok there are also plenty of attractions, although facilities are more basic and the standards of sanitation considerably lower.

Make sure that you pick the dry season to travel (June to August are the best months) and that you allow plenty of time for recuperation and acclimatisation after the long flight. Prior to departure, consult your physician for details of injections and any other necessary precautions that should be taken.

WHAT TO SEE

JAVA: JAKARTA AND SURROUNDINGS
Pasar Burung (Bird Market)
Parrots, doves and other exotic species of birds hang out in bamboo cages in this colourful little market (see page 37).

Pulau Seribu
Sun, sea and sand on dazzling tropical islands all within easy reach of Indonesia's capital city. Bring sun hats and high protection sun-tan oil (see page 48).

Ragunan Zoo
More than 1,000 animals, including the famous Komodo dragon, make this the perfect place for children and weary parents to escape to. Avoid at weekends (see page 32).

Taman Impian Ancol
Countless attractions for children of all ages, ranging from oceanarium to planetarium and jumping dolphins (see pages 38–9).

Taman Mini-Indonesia
Indonesia in miniature with giant snails, pleasure boats, birds and even a model train to take you around the various cultural sights (see page 39).

CENTRAL AND EAST JAVA

Handicraft Villages (Yogya)
Potters, silver-craftsmen and woodcarvers churn out every kind of work of art in these little villages (see page 55).

Pasar Ngasem Bird Market (Yogya)
Turtle doves, chickens and strange-coloured parrots are enough to tickle the fancy of the toughest toddler (see page 54).

Parangtritis
Escape to the seaside with sand dunes and donkey rides, but beware of big waves and dangerous currents (see page 59).

Sarangan
Cool hills, a crater lake filled with paddle boats and waterfalls nearby make this a pleasant retreat from the heat of the plains (see page 142).

Surabaya Zoo
About 500 species of animals and exotic birds, from flying squirrels to dwarf buffalo, can be observed here (see page 71).

BALI

Goa Lawah
Bats by the million live in this legendary cave situated opposite the seafront (see page 85).

Monkey Forest (Ubud)
Hundreds of monkeys scramble up trees and demand to be fed with peanuts and bananas. Be very careful, however, as they can be vicious (see page 117).

Nusa Dua
Bali's most exclusive beach area with sea, sand, swimming pools and security (see page 93).

Petulu
Sit in the rice fields and watch thousands

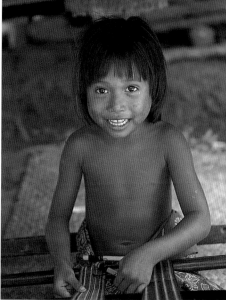
A young Sasak weaver

of egrets nesting in the trees at sunset. Situated near Ubud (see pages 114–15).

Sanur Beach
Fine beaches and a touch of luxury away from the crowds (see pages 82–3).

Uluwatu Temple
Hundreds of energetic monkeys, sheer cliffs and the crashing of waves below make this a popular family outing, but beware the enthusiasm of the monkeys (see pages 92–3).

LOMBOK

Sade Village
Thatched houses and rice farmers, with weavers merrily churning out tourist items (see page 128).

Senggigi Beach
Sun, sea and sand with good hotels and boat trips in the vicinity (see page 127).

Tetebatu
Cool mountain air, rice fields and horses and carts make this Lombok's perfect inland base for short walks and tours (see pages 128–9).

A smile for everyone

Sport

*I*n the heat of Indonesia's midday sun you would be foolish to exert yourself too much. Still, there are plenty of opportunities for golfing, swimming and sailing that will provide both relaxation and exercise. And for the less energetic, there is no shortage of spectator sports, from bull racing to scorpion fighting. For details of current sporting events enquire at the relevant tourist offices.

BULL RACING
You may have to visit the island of Madura to witness this exciting spectator sport (see page 75), but *aficionados* claim that it is definitely worth the trouble. The race involves two beautifully decorated bulls hurtling down a football pitch faster than Carl Lewis, tagging along 13-year-old boys on planks. There's plenty of excitement, too, from the bulls who are fed rice wine to lift their spirits and psyched up by the sounds of a *gamelan* orchestra. Competitions are held between August and September but enquire locally as locations vary from day to day.

COCK-FIGHTING
Bali is the place where you are most likely to encounter this activity. Although the government has banned cock-fights, the Balinese flout the laws with contempt. Have no doubts about the barbarous nature of this 'sport'; specially trained and manicured cocks attack one another with pecker and claws carrying razor blades in a raucous flutter of feathers that may only last a matter of seconds. Numerous observers place bets on the outcome.

DIVING, see Getting Away From it All, page 144.

GOLF
One of Indonesia's newly discovered sports, golf is fast becoming one of the country's biggest attractions. The scenery is second to none, courses are of a good standard, green rates are relatively low and caddies easy to come by. If you intend to play at weekends, however, book in advance. Courses within easy reach of the capital are the Jakarta Golf Club (tel: 489 1208), Pondok Indah Golf & Country Club (tel: 769 4906) and Sunter Golf Plain (tel: 491 799). For the best that Indonesia has to offer, travel to the Handara Country Club, near Bedugal on the island of Bali (tel: 288 66), ranked as one of the 50 most beautiful golf courses in the world.

RAM FIGHTING
This is one of the unlikeliest 'sports' that anyone could ever dream up but, cruelty aside, ram fighting is big business, especially in Bandung and other towns in West Java. Typically, two hyped-up rams charge blindly at one another to the sound of drums and gongs and the raucous cries of the locals, who place bets. Only when one of the animals is knocked out is the winner declared and two new specimens lined up for the next bout.

SAILING
Several companies now organise sailing holidays around Bali and Java ranging from just a day's outing to several weeks.

Above: watersports in Benoa
Right: paragliding on Bali

You can take your pick from an old schooner or a modern cruiser, and enjoy some of the most spectacular marine scenery in the East. For details contact: P & O Spice Island Cruises, Jalan Jen Parmen 78, Slipi, Jakarta Barat (tel: (021) 593 401/2). Also see pages 136–7.

SURFING
Indonesia is ideal for surfing, although you should watch out for strong undercurrents which take their toll every year. Beginners and intermediate surfers flock to Kuta Beach on Bali. Experienced surfers opt for Uluwatu (Pantai Suluban), a short distance to the south (see page 90).

SWIMMING AND TENNIS
Almost all the big hotels have swimming pools. Some have tennis courts, Jacuzzis and fitness centres. If you are not a hotel guest, you can generally pay to use the facilities.

OTHER SPORTS
Boating, mountaineering, trekking and riding are all popular sporting activities in Indonesia, along with less adventurous pursuits such as table tennis, badminton and bowling. For something a little different, you can even take an 8-day cycle tour around Lombok with Bidy Tours (tel: 0364 22127), or paraglide over the sparkling bay of Bali's Benoa Beach, north of Nusa Dua.

Food and Drink

*I*f you go to Indonesia expecting a gastronomic treat, you may find yourself disappointed. For while the country does offer a variety of delicious foods, the cuisine cannot for the most part compare with that of neighbouring countries.

Almost every meal revolves around *nasi* (rice), with the addition of vegetables, peanuts or dried fish. Indeed, if there is a national meal, then it is probably *nasi goreng*, a mixture of fried rice, meat and onions with occasionally a fried egg perched on top.

Most dishes use spices like garlic and ginger, but not liberally. Sometimes you may come across that most beloved of all Asian culinary additives, the deadly *cabe* (chilli), nestling surreptitiously under a mound of rice or turned into *sambal*, a

sauce made with lime and brown paste. If you do take a mouthful of fire, the best way to cool it is neither water nor beer, but plain rice or a squirt of lime juice. To avoid this possibility, simply say *jangan terlalu pedas* ('not too spicy please').

As a rule Indonesians eat informally. If you are invited to somebody's house, however, remember never to finish your rice as this suggests that you have not been fed sufficiently. Use the right hand to pass food (the left is considered unclean) and wait for your host to start eating or drinking before you tuck in.

A TYPICAL MENU
Outside the big tourist centres of Kuta, Sanur, Nusa Dua and Jakarta, don't expect to find garnished steak and chips on the menu. A more likely alternative is *nasi rames*, which consists of white rice, meat or fish and vegetables, or *cap cay*, a delicious mixture of stir-fried vegetables with garlic.

If that does not suit, you can normally order *soto*, a thick soup with coconut milk, served with *krupuk*, which are large prawn crackers.

Gado gado is another popular local dish and is made up of half-cooked salad served with a spicy peanut sauce. Elsewhere there's plenty of *mi goreng*,

Street market, Bedulu

Red chillies have the heat of a furnace and the kick of a water buffalo

which is fried wheat flour noodles, or *nasi lemak*, which is rice with coconut milk, anchovies, egg and cucumber.

For dessert, Indonesians eat a variety of glutinous rice cakes often known as *jaja*. These are made from dough mixed with grated coconut, sweet potato or banana. If that is not to your taste, try *rumak*, made up of crisp, unripe fruit in a sweet and sour sauce, or simply ask for those delicious *pisang goreng* (fried bananas).

JAVANESE CUISINE

Although you will find rice served almost everywhere in Indonesia, each town and each region in the country also boasts its own speciality, with the *pièce de résistance* being fried worms and dragonflies.

In West Java, especially, Sundanese food is likely to feature on the menu. Popular dishes include *pepes usus* (chicken steamed in bamboo leaf), as

well as spiced buffalo meat. For something a little different, order a plate of *petei* (spicy broad-bean salad) or *soto Bandung* (soup made from tripe).

In Central Java, and especially in Yogyakarta, the biggest speciality is a dish called *gudeg*, made from rice with boiled jack fruit, mixed with chicken, egg, coconut, cream and spicy sauce. *Ayam goreng* (chicken fried with spices and coconut) is another favourite, which is served with sweet chilli and rice. More adventurous eaters can opt for *opor* (barbecued sheep's brain)

In East Java, and especially Madura, soups are common, especially *soto madura* (spicy chicken broth). Almost everywhere you will come across *warungs* (food stalls) selling Padang food from West Sumatra. The food is cold, on occasions fiercesomely hot, but absolutely delicious. Added to that you are charged only for the dishes you eat.

BALINESE CUISINE

On Bali you can feast on roasted pig as well as steaks, fruits and almost every form of Western cuisine. Added to that is wonderful seafood freshly caught off the island's sparkling beaches.

If you fancy a *babi guling* (roasted pig), order it the night before to allow the restaurateur to prepare the pig for you by stuffing it with a spice-leaf mixture and then roasting it over a fire.

Another speciality is *betutu bebek*, a dish that consists of a whole duck stuffed with spices, wrapped in leaves then either steamed or roasted.

Other popular snacks on Bali range from unripe fruit to rice cakes.

OTHER CUISINES

Whilst nobody should miss an opportunity to try these exotic local titbits, there's no shortage of other Western restaurants in the main towns for those who do not take to such gastronomic novelties. Thai, Vietnamese, French, Italian and Indian food can be found in Jakarta, although at prices that are four or five times higher than local fare. In addition, almost all the major hotels will have Western-style restaurants. Certainly nobody should miss out on the traditional Dutch *rijstaffel*. This literally means 'rice table' and describes a whole banquet of side dishes such as kebabs and fried prawns.

STREET STALLS

Some of the most delicious food is to be found not in the five-star restaurants but in the humble little *warungs* (food stalls) or *rumah makan* (eating houses) which are frequented by appreciative locals.

Above, left: street vendor, Yogyakarta
Left: candies for sale, Bali

From noodles to Kebabs, Indonesia has plenty of fast food to offer

These *warungs* serve a variety of rice dishes or noodles as well as *satay* (kebabs), usually made from goat's meat and barbecued on a charcoal fire. To choose, just point at any dish that takes your fancy, sit down and feast on some of the cheapest and tastiest food that Indonesia has to offer. If you are nervous about your constitution, wait a few days before you venture out to the local stalls and always make sure that the food is freshly cooked.

DRINKS

You can drink Coca Cola or Fanta, or occasionally even expensive wine in the main towns of Bali, Java and Lombok, but the one thing that you should never miss out on is fruit shakes. These, made with papaya, pineapple, banana, lime and all the other luscious fruits that grow around the archipelago, can be bought from many restaurants catering for tourists and are the perfect antidote to a hot steamy day. To avoid stomach problems, ask for no ice (*tanpa es*).

For something a little stronger, Indonesia serves several good beers such as Heineken or the locally brewed Bintang, which was introduced by the Dutch. Finally, to avoid dehydration, drink as much water as possible. You can buy bottles of water in the shops or restaurants, although more up-market hotels will provide jugs of boiled water. Never, under any circumstances, drink tap water, which even the locals view with suspicion.

WHERE TO EAT

Eating in Indonesia is almost universally cheap. A good local meal will generally cost less than Rp10,000 a head (excluding alcohol) and only in the European restaurants in the big hotels will the cost be higher.

In the restaurant listings below, the following symbols have been used to indicate the average cost per person, not including alcohol.

R = Rp4,000–Rp10,000
RR = Rp10,000–Rp20,000
RRR = Rp 20,000–Rp40,000

Service is generally charged at the rate of 10 per cent in the bigger restaurants. Otherwise it is generally sufficient to leave Rp500 or Rp1,000 on the table as a tip.

JAKARTA
Indonesian Food
Club Noordwijk RRR
Dutch and Indonesian food, colonial atmosphere.
Jalan Ir Juanda 5A (tel: 353 909).
Nelayan Seafood Restaurant RR
Fine seafood in crowded setting.
Manggala Wanabakti Building, Jalan Gatot Subroto (tel: 570 0248).
Oasis Restaurant RRR
Gourmet food served in a magnificent turn-of-the-century mansion. Speciality: *rijstaffel* (around 15 dishes served on antique plates).
Jalan Radan Saleh 47 (tel: 326 397).
Sari Kuring R
Popular Indonesian food and seafood.
Silang Monas Timur 88 (tel: 384 1542).
Sari Bundo RR
One of the best Padang-food restaurants in town.
Jalan Haji Juanda 27 (tel: 358 343).
Satay House Senayan R
Renowned for its *gado gado* and *satay*

(barbecued kebabs).
Jalan Kebon Sirih 31A (tel: 326 239).
Yun Njan RR
One of Jakarta's best-known seafood restaurants.
Jalan Batuceper 69, near Jalan Hayam Wuruk (tel: 364 063).

European Food
Ambiente Italian Restaurant RRR
Finest Italian cuisine in Jakarta.
Aryaduta Hotel, Jalan Prapatan 44–46 (tel: 376 008).
George & Dragon RR
English/Indian food in popular expat establishment.
Jalan Teluk Betung 32 (tel: 325 625).
Le Bistro RR
Bouillabaisse, *entrecôte* and some of the best French food in town.
Jalan Wahid Hasyim 75 (tel: 364 272).
Memories RRR
Dutch cuisine with colonial trappings.
Wisma Indocement, Jalan Sudirman 70–71 (tel: 578 1008).
The Ponderoso RR
Large steaks, salads and Mexican food are on the menu.
Lippo Centre, Jalan Gatot Subroto 35–36 (tel: 520 0480).

Indian Food
Mutu Curry RR
Spicy Indian dishes served on banana leaves.
Jalan Tanah Abang Timur 14 (tel: 380 5233).

YOGYAKARTA
Indonesian Food
Hanoman's Forest Garden Restaurant RR
Indonesian and Western food with classical Javanese dance.
Jalan Prawirotaman 9B.

Palm House R
Extremely popular, with Indonesian, Chinese and Western food.
Jalan Prawirotaman.
Pesta Perak R
Wide selection of Javanese dishes and small garden.
Jalan Tentara Rakyat Mataram 8 (tel: 55231).
Suharti's Ayam Goreng R
Specialises in fried chicken, the regional delicacy.
Jalan Laksda Adisucipto 208 (tel: 5522).

European Food
French Grill RRR
Popular French food with classical dance or puppet shows.
Arjuna Plaza Hotel, Jalan Mangkubuni 48 (tel: 86862).
Gita Buana RR
Delicious steaks, European dishes and Chinese fare.
Jalan Adisucipto 89 (tel: 61164).
Legian Garden Restaurant RR
Delightfully situated with good Western and local food.
Jalan Perwakilan 9 (tel: 87985).
Superman's R
Pancakes, yoghurts and Indonesian dishes for backpackers.
Gang Sosrowijayan I (runs parallel with Marlboro).

SURABAYA
Indonesian Food
Antika R
Reputedly the best Padang food in town.
Jalan Raya Darmo 1.
Bon Café RR
Variety of Indonesian and Chinese dishes and ice creams.
Jalan Raya Gubeng 46 (tel: 42309).
Soto Ambengan R
Famous for its Madurese chicken soup

with lemon grass.
Jalan Ambengan 3A.

European Food
Angus House Charcoal Steak Grill RR
World Trade Centre, 6th floor, Jalan Pemuda 26–31 (tel: 519 282).
Café Venezia RR
Jalan Ambengan 16 (tel: 43091).
Satellite Garden RR
Jalan Raya Kupang Baru 17.

BALI
Kuta Beach
Made's Warung R
Popular Indonesian and Western food, relaxed atmosphere.
Jalan Pantai Kuta (tel: 51923).
Poppies R
Delightful setting, consistently good food.
Jalan Legian (tel: 51059).

Sanur Beach
Bali Moon RR
Italian food in open-air setting.
Jalan Tamblingan 19.
Kul Kul RR
Excellent Indonesian and Western food in garden setting.
Jalan Danau Tamblingan 166 (tel: 88038).
Tanjung Sari Hotel Restaurant RRR
One of the most exquisite restaurants on the island.
Jalan Tanjung Sari (tel: 8351).

Ubud
Lotus Restaurant RR
Good food, delightful setting.
Jalan Raya, next to Pura Saraswati (tel: 95363).
Murni's Warung R
Fine fruit salads, yoghurts and a huge variety of Western and local fare.
Jalan Raya (near Tjampuhan Bridge).

Hotels and Accommodation

*I*ndonesia has some of the top hotels in the world, with swimming pools, restaurants and tropical gardens to match. At the lower end of the scale it has some of the friendliest homestays where you can stay with a family for less than US$5 a night.

Prices vary as much as the establishments. In Jakarta, a top suite at the Grand Hyatt Hotel will cost as much as US$600, whilst in the less exclusive hotels around the corner, standard rooms go for US$50–US$100. Outside Jakarta prices are considerably lower, while on Bali you will find a bewildering choice of accommodation to suit every pocket.

Remember that in the high season (June to September), when the vast majority of Europeans take their holidays, it can be extremely hard finding accommodation if you turn up without a reservation. At other times of year it is quite possible to negotiate big discounts.

Tariffs are generally quoted in Indonesian *rupiah*, except in the big hotels where US dollars are the norm. A 15.5 per cent tax along with various service charges may be added, but enquire on arrival.

DO'S AND DON'TS

Although finding a satisfactory hotel in Indonesia is little different from finding one in any other country, there are a few points that are worth remembering.

The key to an enjoyable stay is a

❖

THOMAS COOK
Traveller's Tip

Travellers who purchase their travel tickets from a Thomas Cook network location are entitled to use the services of any other Thomas Cook network location, free of charge, to make hotel reservations.

---

central location, especially in Jakarta where a hotel on the outskirts may entail hours in a traffic jam. If you are making an advance reservation through a travel agent, always double-check the address, as often what you are told is central proves to be quite a distance from where you want to be. Generally, it is worth paying a little more to be close to the tourist sites.

Cheaper establishments in big towns tend to be dirty and noisy; sometimes, the small Chinese hotels may even double up as brothels. If you end up staying in a less than desirable establishment, make sure that you take security precautions and carry valuables in a money belt.

To be on the safe side, always arrive at your destination early to allow time to find a place to stay. Remember that the word hotel generally indicates a more expensive establishment, while the word *losmen* refers to a lower-price hotel or guesthouse.

Don't be afraid to check out the bedrooms and bathrooms and to ask for something larger or cleaner if what is on offer does not suit your taste. Many hotels will have several different standards of room with corresponding prices to match. Sometimes, you may even get breakfast included.

Never, under any circumstances, drink water from the tap. Most big hotels will provide jugs of boiled water. Finally, remember that phone calls and hotel meals are expensive, and that hotels add a hefty service charge to the bill.

SHOPPING AROUND

Although most hotels of a similar price bracket will offer comparable standards, it is always worth shopping around. Taxi or *becak* (tricycle) drivers are generally happy to take you to a selection of hotels because if you take a room they may get commission. At major airports like Jakarta and Denpasar special hotel reservation desks offer the full range of accommodation.

Right: five-star accommodation, Bali
Below: tropical comfort, Sanur Beach, Bali

PRICES AND FACILITIES

BALI

All the big international hotel chains like Hyatt and Sheraton are to be found on Bali, along with plenty of clean and pleasant hotels and homestays *(losmen)*. Although prices at the top tend to be on a par with other international destinations, at the lower end simple, clean accommodation goes for a song.

Deluxe

Most of the deluxe accommodation is situated in the coastal areas and especially in the resorts of Nusa Dua and Sanur. Top-class hotels have every amenity from luxuriant gardens to swimming pools, fitness centres and restaurants. Almost all of them organise tours and will be able to arrange chauffeur-driven cars.

Rates can be as high as US$500 for a suite at the Amanpuri, although most luxury establishments in Nusa Dua charge in the region of US$100-US$150 a night. Off season, however, you may be able to negotiate considerably lower prices. For peace of mind, book early, especially if you intend to stay during peak season.

Standard

Even mid-priced hotels and bungalows on Bali generally offer swimming pools and charming little gardens, as well as restaurants and travel services. Standard hotels vary in price from Rp40,000 to Rp100,000, although prices may be considerably lower during the low season.

Budget

Budget hotels and *losmen* (homestays) are found literally everywhere on Bali, offering clean and simple accommodation at bargain prices. In Ubud, prices for a small family owned *losmen* with a private *mandi* (a water tank from which to ladle water over yourself) can start as low as Rp6,000, breakfast included. These *losmen* are generally extremely friendly and a fine source of local information. Although security is generally high, always keep an eye on your belongings.

JAVA

Although hotels on Java as a rule cannot match those on Bali, Jakarta does have all the luxury amenities of any capital city – at a price. Outside the major tourist centres, standards tend to be considerably lower, with many small towns sporting little more than dingy Chinese hotels with an abundance of cockroaches.

Deluxe

From the Grand Hyatt to the Borobudur and the Mandarin Oriental, Jakarta has the full range of five-star accommodation with prices beginning at around US$100 per night before taxes. Outside Jakarta prices and standards are considerably lower. Make reservations well in advance as growing numbers of businessmen have led to high rates of occupancy.

Standard

There is not a huge amount to choose from in the standard range, except in the bigger cities which have plenty of mid-priced accommodation. Expect to pay between Rp60,000 and Rp100,000 in Jakarta and considerably less outside.

Budget

If you think you have stayed in some rough places in Asia, some of Java's basement accommodation can give you a run for your money. Rooms can be dingy in the extreme and security extremely poor. Prices range from as low as

Living in the lap of luxury at Jakarta's Grand Hyatt Hotel

Rp6,000, although you will pay higher rates in Jakarta. To find a satisfactory establishment, inspect the various rooms, and if you don't like any of them simply move on somewhere else.

LOMBOK

Until recently, Lombok offered little in the way of tourist accommodation but these days there is a Sheraton Hotel on Senggigi Beach, as well as several other luxury developments, plus a handful of cheaper establishments. Outside Senggigi accommodation tends to be basic and although there are several bungalows on the Gili Islands, and at Kuta and Tetebatu, there are fewer and generally less impressive ones elsewhere.

On Business

Fifteen years ago Jakarta was one of the most chaotic business centres in the whole of Asia. These days, it not only offers access to one of the fastest-growing economies in the world, but has the attractions of a relatively progressive city.

Here you will find foreign banks and plenty of multi-national corporations. On top of that, there is an active stock market known as the Jakarta Stock Exchange, a nascent bond market and an extremely fast-growing business community.

Outside Jakarta, the only other real business centre is Surabaya which now serves the eastern part of the Indonesian archipelago and has become the focal point of the government's efforts to decentralise the economy. Surabaya has a big Chinese community, a selection of leading manufacturing concerns, and a private stock exchange.

ACCOMMODATION

Business accommodation in Jakarta is plentiful with at least five major hotels offering every conceivable amenity. Prices for the top suites are in line with other business centres around the world and service of a high standard. To ensure room availability, book in advance.

BUREAUCRACY

If you are expecting to obtain a major business decision on your first trip to Indonesia, prepare to be disappointed. Doing business takes time and effort; much of it is a question of face, and at almost every level vast amounts of paper work and endless discussions with the country's notorious bureaucracy may be involved. The only real way to avoid hassles is to establish a joint venture with a reputable local partner. For details about investment requirements and government incentives, contact the

Indonesian Investment Co-ordinating Board (BKPM) in Jakarta (tel: 520 2047).

BUSINESS ETIQUETTE

Indonesian businessmen pride themselves on their appearance. They generally wear a suit and tie and expect visiting foreigners to do the same. Always shake hands and offer a business card, and when addressing a businessman use his full title. Initially you should expect to spend several hours in discussion, as long, drawn-out negotiations are usual. Any initial contact may skirt around the key issues which will often require further discussions.

If you are offered the opportunity of lunch or dinner, it is considered impolite to turn down the invitation. These days, breakfast meetings are on the increase. If you are the host in Jakarta, choose between the Grand Hyatt, the Mandarin, the Borobudur or the Hilton. Smaller hotels will be viewed as a reflection of inferior status.

BUSINESS TRANSPORT

All the big hotels offer a limousine service, charged either by the day or by the hour. Chauffeurs will take you to an appointment and pick you up later in the day. Bluebird taxis are also available and can be rented by the hour at considerably cheaper rates.

COMMUNICATIONS

Computers, printers, fax machines and photocopiers can be found in all the major hotels. Costs of hiring computers (generally by the hour) are, however, high. Local telephone services have improved dramatically over the last five years, but remain poor by Western standards. International calls on the other hand can be made very quickly and easily.

CONFERENCE AND EXHIBITION FACILITIES

Most of the big hotels offer conference and exhibition facilities catering for from 30 to several hundred guests. Contact the following for details:

Grand Hyatt Hotel, *Plaza Indonesia, Jalan Thamrin (tel: 3107 400)*.

Hilton Hotel, *Jalan Jend Subroto (tel: 587 981)*.

Borobudur Hotel, *Jalan Lapangan Banteng Selatan (tel: 370 333)*.

Mandarin Oriental Hotel, *Jalan Thamrin (tel: 321 307)*.

MEDIA

Several weekly publications offer local business news. These include the *Review Indonesia* and the *Indonesia Business Weekly*. The daily English-language newspapers are the *Jakarta Post* and the *Indonesian Observer*. All the big hotels sell the *International Herald Tribune*, the *Asian Wall Street Journal* and

the *Financial Times*, although you may find them a few days out of date.

OFFICE HOURS

Offices generally open between 9am and 5pm from Mondays to Fridays, although financial service companies may begin as early as 8am and close as late as 6pm. On Saturdays, many non-government offices in Jakarta are open for a half day. All offices are closed on Sundays.

SECRETARIAL AND TRANSLATION SERVICES

Secretarial and translation services are widely available in leading hotels. Costs are generally in line with other international business centres.

A selection of indonesian tabloids

Practical Guide

CONTENTS

ARRIVING

Entry Formalities

Visitors to Indonesia must be in possession of passports valid for at least six months from the date of arrival and have proof of onward or return passage. Visas for a stay of up to 60 days are automatically granted on arrival to nationals of the UK, Australia, New Zealand and Canada. Nationals from South Africa will need a visa.

Travellers who require visas should obtain them in their country of residence, as it may prove difficult to obtain them elsewhere. In the UK, Thomas Cook Passport and Visa Service can advise on and obtain the necessary documentation. Consult your nearest Thomas Cook travel consultant.

By Air

Indonesia's major international gateway is Soekarno-Hatta International Airport in Jakarta, which is served by airlines from Europe, North America, Australia and the Middle East, as well as by Garuda, the national flag carrier. Facilities are of a high standard, with banks, car rental, telephones, tourist information, left luggage, and even a hotel reservation service.

These days, an increasing number of tourists fly directly to Denpasar's Ngurah Rai International Airport on Bali. Flights arrive and depart from Amsterdam, Singapore, Hong Kong, Kuala Lumpur and Perth in Western Australia.

If you intend to fly during the high season, make sure that you reserve a seat early, and on the return trip remember to reconfirm your flight at least 72 hours prior to departure.

Tax: an airport tax of Rp17,500 is charged on departure for international flights and Rp3,500 on domestic flights.

To and From Jakarta Airport: a fleet of taxis connects Soekarno-Hatta International Airport with the centre of Jakarta, which lies 14km to the west. Fares are in the region of Rp28,000, including toll charges, and only if you take an expensive air-conditioned limousine will it cost you much more. During the week the journey should take 40 minutes to the centre of town, although to be safe allow more than an hour.

Airport buses depart every 30 minutes for the Gambir Train Station and Blok M in Kebayoran, as well as for various other points in the city where there are taxi connections.

To and From Denpasar Airport (Bali): taxis will take you from Ngurah Rai International Airport, which lies a short distance from Denpasar, to Sanur in less than 20 minutes and to Kuta in 15 minutes. Public buses run to the centre of town at frequent intervals.

By Ship

Although not a popular method of entry, several luxury passenger vessels do sail between Singapore, Hong Kong, Jakarta and Bali, including the *Pearl of Scandinavia* and the *Coral Princess*. You can also catch boats from Singapore to the island of Sumatra. At Jakarta, boats berth at Tanjung Priok Harbour, 10km to the northeast of the city.

CAMPING

You will find opportunities for camping in several of the national parks but otherwise camping is not recommended. At best you may find yourself being woken up by a herd of inquisitive water buffalo, at worst by a group of locals who may be after more than your guy ropes.

CHILDREN

Up-market tourist hotels can generally arrange babysitters. Nappies are sold in shops and department stores in all the major cities. See also Children, pages 160–1.

Soekarno-Hatta International Airport

Sunny days in Padangbai, Bali

CLIMATE

May through to October are the best months to visit Java, Bali and Lombok as for the most part the weather is dry with only short bouts of rain in the early and latter parts. November to April is the monsoon season when tropical downpours alternate with sunshine. January and February are generally the wettest months of the year. Average temperatures are between 25°C and 28°C, but this may drop to 18°C or lower in the mountainous areas. Average humidity is 75 per cent. On Bali the rains tend to last longer, with the greatest concentration of sun between July and October.

CLOTHING, see page 25.

CONVERSION TABLES, see opposite

CRIME

Like any developing country, crime is on the rise in Indonesia, especially in

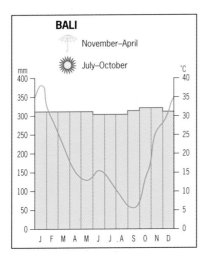

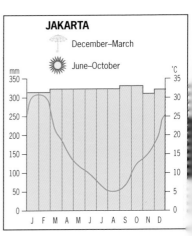

Conversion Table

FROM	TO	MULTIPLY BY
Inches	Centimetres	2.54
Feet	Metres	0.3048
Yards	Metres	0.9144
Miles	Kilometres	1.6090
Acres	Hectares	0.4047
Gallons	Litres	4.5460
Ounces	Grams	28.35
Pounds	Grams	453.6
Pounds	Kilograms	0.4536
Tons	Tonnes	1.0160

To convert back, for example from centimetres to inches, divide by the number in the the third column.

Men's Suits

UK	36	38	40	42	44	46	48
Rest of Europe	46	48	50	52	54	56	58
US	36	38	40	42	44	46	48

Dress Sizes

UK	8	10	12	14	16	18
France	36	38	40	42	44	46
Italy	38	40	42	44	46	48
Rest of Europe	34	36	38	40	42	44
US	6	8	10	12	14	16

Men's Shirts

UK	14	14.5	15	15.5	16	16.5	17
Rest of Europe	36	37	38 39/40	41		42	43
US	14	14.5	15	15.5	16	16.5	17

Men's Shoes

UK	7	7.5 8.5	9.5	10.5	11
Rest of Europe	41	42 43	44	45	46
US	8	8.5 9.5	10.5	11.5	12

Women's Shoes

UK	4.5	5	5.5	6	6.5	7
Rest of Europe	38	38	39	39	40	41
US	6	6.5	7	7.5	8	8.5

the big cities where pick-pockets and small-time thieves are commonplace. To protect yourself, make sure that you never carry around large amounts of cash or ostentatious jewellery, and use a money belt and the hotel safe.

Women should avoid travelling alone, especially on Java and Lombok. Locals regard single women as easy game and will pester them throughout their journey.

CUSTOMS REGULATIONS

The following items may be taken duty free into Indonesia: 2 litres of alcohol, 200 cigarettes or 50 cigars or 100 grams of tobacco. In principle, cassette recorders, typewriters and photographic equipment must be declared upon entry, although in practice customs officers will wave you through. All narcotics, arms and ammunition are prohibited. It is advisable to fully label all tablets and first-aid items, and to carry proof of purchase with you at all times.

Drugs

Possession or consumption of drugs is an extremely serious offence in Indonesia, punishable by life imprisonment. Never accept a package from any stranger, whoever they may claim to be, and never even consider smuggling drugs into or out of the country.

DISABLED TRAVELLERS

Besides lifts at the big hotels and wheelchairs at the international and domestic airports provided by Garuda, there is little in the way of facilities for disabled travellers in Indonesia.

ATTENTION

I. THOSE WHO ARE NOT ALLOWED TO ENTER THE TEMPLE ARE:
1. LADIES WHO ARE PREGNANT
2. LADIES WHOSE CHILDREN HAVE NOT GOT THE FIRST TEETH
3. CHILDREN WHOSE FIRST TEETH NOT FALLEN OUT YET
4. LADIES DURING THEIR PERIOD
5. DVOTEES GETTING IMPURE DUE TO DEATH
6. MAD LADIES / GENTLEMEN
7. THOSE NOT PROPERLY DRESSED
II. ALL DVOTEES ENTERING THE TEMPLE SHOULD MAINTAIN CLEANLINESS AND ENVIRONMENTAL CONSERVATION

Signs of the times

DRIVING

In theory, driving offers the perfect opportunity to escape the crowds. In practice, you may find Indonesian drivers to be among the worst in the world, especially in Jakarta which is a mad-house of traffic jams and one-way streets.

Few foreigners even bother to drive in the capital, preferring if necessary to hire a driver. On Bali and Lombok driving does make more sense, however, although even here nonchalant water buffalo and speeding buses can challenge even the most experienced drivers.

Those who do decide to take the plunge will need an international driving licence. You will also require insurance, although most reliable rental firms will be able to arrange this on the spot.

As a rule, main roads on Bali and Lombok are in a relatively good state of repair, although during the rainy season non-tarmac roads will be literally awash. Vehicles drive on the right (generally) with major towns signposted in English.

Petrol stations are few and far between, so always top up when you get the opportunity. Failing that, stop by one of the ubiquitous roadside stalls selling gasoline by the litre bottle.

Car Hire

Car-hire firms exist in many of the larger towns. To be safe, opt for a well-known international firm.

Jakarta

Avis Car Rental, *Jalan Diponegoro 25, Jakarta 10310 (tel: 334 495).*

Hertz Car Rental, *Plaza Podium, Jalan Jend Sudirman (tel: 570 3683).*

Toyota Rentacar, *Jalan Hasyim Ashari 31, Jakarta (tel: 362 672).*

Bali

Avis, *Bali Hyatt Hotel, Sanur Beach (tel: 88271).*

National Car Rental, *Bali Beach Hotel (tel: 88511).*

Bicycle and Moped Hire

Bicycles and motorcycles can prove the perfect way to explore the countryside, so long as you can put up with the heat and the dust. On Bali, in Surakarta (Solo) and Yogyakarta especially, bicycles are relatively easy to come by, while in Kuta you may even find mountain bikes now. Daily rates are generally low but it is better to negotiate by the week. Before you depart, check that the bicycle or moped is in proper working order as you will be liable for any damage, and make sure that you lock the bicycle/motorbike at all times. Although insurance is not a legal requirement, everyone should make it a pre-requisite as accidents are by no means uncommon.

ELECTRICITY

Power supply is generally 220 volts in the big cities, but 110 volts is still used in some areas. Normal outlets take plugs with two rounded prongs. If in doubt, take an electrical adaptor.

EMBASSIES AND CONSULATES

The following is an abbreviated list of embassies and consulates in Jakarta. For a full list, see the telephone directory or any of the free hand-outs issued by the tourist authorities.

Australia, *15 Jalan Thamrin, Jakarta (tel: 323 109).*
Canada, *Wisma Metropolitan 1, 5th floor, Jalan Jend Sudirman 29, Jakarta (tel: 510 709).*
Great Britain, *75 Jalan Thamrin, Jakarta (tel: 330 904).*
New Zealand, *41 Jalan Diponegoro, Menteng, Jakarta (tel: 330 680).*
United States, *5 Jalan Merdeka Selatan, Jakarta (tel: 360 360).*

EMERGENCY TELEPHONE NUMBERS

Jakarta
Ambulance: 118 or 334 030
Fire: 113
Police: 110

Bali
Ambulance: 118 or 27911
Fire: 113
Police: 110

Jakarta Hospitals
Gatot Subroto Hospital, *Jalan Abdul Rachman Saleh (tel: 371 008).*
Pertamina Hospital, *Jalan Kyai Maja 43 (tel: 775 890 or 775 891).*
Rumah Sakit Pondok Indah, *Jalan Metro Duta 1 (tel: 767 525)* – operates a 24-hour emergency service.

Bali Hospitals
Sanglah Public Hospital, *Jalan Kesehatan 1, Sanglah, Denpasar (tel: (0361) 27911).*
Wangaya Public Hospital, *Jalan Kartini, Denpasar (tel: 22141).*

Dharma Usaha Clinic, *Jalan Sudirman 50, Denpasar (tel: 27544).*

The Thomas Cook Worldwide Customer Promise offers free emergency assistance at any Thomas Cook Network location to travellers who have purchased their travel tickets at a Thomas Cook location. In addition, any MasterCard cardholder may use any Thomas Cook Network location to report loss or theft of their card and obtain an emergency card replacement as a free service under Thomas Cook MasterCard International Alliance.

Thomas Cook travellers' cheque refund (24-hour service – report loss or theft within 24 hours): tel: (44) 733 502995.

Bejac driver, Jakarta

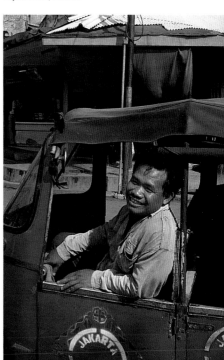

HEALTH

There are no mandatory vaccination requirements for visiting Indonesia, but vaccination against tetanus, polio, typhoid and hepatitis A is recommended. Coastal areas are free of malaria, but anti-malarial tablets are advised for travellers intending to stay in inland rural areas either overnight or for longer periods of time.

Strict food and water hygiene is essential to avoid problems with diarrhoea. Make sure food has been properly washed and prepared and drink bottled water only (which means avoiding ice cubes).

Aids is present in Indonesia as elsewhere in the world, along with a host of other venereal diseases.

For the most part, the big hotels can arrange for a doctor to call or arrange hospital treatment. Jakarta and Denpasar have good medical facilities but in very remote places the only real alternative is to transport the person to the nearest big town.

Up-to-date health advice can be obtained from your Thomas Cook travel consultant or direct from the Thomas Cook Travel Clinic, 45 Berkeley Street, London W1A 1EB (tel: 071 408 4157). This is open for consultation without appointment Monday to Friday, 8.30am–5.30pm, and can give vaccinations, as well as supplying medical advice and a range of first-aid and travel health items.

HITCH-HIKING

Although occasionally visitors may find themselves being offered a free lift by locals, hitch-hiking is not a recommended way of getting around. What is more, since the cost of public transport is extremely low and most towns are served by buses or *bemos*, it is just not worth the risk.

BASIC PHRASES

Basics

Please	**Silakan**
Thank you	**Terima kasih**
Good morning	**Selamat pagi**
Good afternoon	**Selamat siang**
Good evening	**Selamat malam**
Good-bye	**Selamat tinggal**
Excuse me	**Permisi**
Welcome	**Selamat datang**
I don't understand	**Saya tidak mengerti**

Questions

What is your name?	**Siapa nama saudara?**
Where are you from?	**Dari mana?**
How much?	**Berapa?**
Do you speak English?	**Bisa berbicara bahasa Inggris?**
Do you understand?	**Mengerti?**
Where is?	**Dimana ada?**
When?	**Kapan?**

Places

Alley	**Gang**
Airport	**Lapangan terbang**
Beach	**Pantai**
Bus terminal	**Terminal bis**
Hospital	**Rumah Sakit**

INSURANCE

Anybody spending time in Indonesia should arrange insurance prior to departure. Ideally this should cover lost or stolen cash and credit cards as well as guaranteeing a return ticket in case of emergency. Make sure that you get additional cover if items like cameras or videos exceed the individual limit.

Food & Drink			
Hotel	**Hotel**		
Market	**Pasar**	Beef	**Daging Sapi**
Mountain	**Gunung**	Chicken	**Ayam**
Restaurant	**Rumah makan**	Pork	**Babi**
River	**Sungai**	Fish	**Ikan**
Street	**Jalan**	Egg	**Telur**
Temple	**Candi**	Vegetables	**Sayur**
Village	**Desa**	Mixed vegetables	**Cap cai**
		Noodles	**Mie**
Time		Fried noodles	**Mie Goreng**
Yesterday	**Kemarin**	Rice	**Nasi**
Today	**Hari ini**	Fried rice	**Nasi Goreng**
Tomorrow	**Besok**	Soup	**Sop/soto**
Hour	**Jam**	Fruit	**Buah**
Week	**Minggu**	Beer	**Bir**
Month	**Bulan**	Boiled water	**Air putih**
Year	**Tahun**	Coffee	**Kopi**
		Milk	**Susu**
Useful Words		Tea	**Teh**
Bathroom	**Kamar Mandi**	Sugar	**Gula**
Cheap	**Murah**		
Drink	**Minum**	**Numbers**	
Eat	**Makan**	One	**Satu**
Expensive	**Mahal**	Two	**Dua**
Good	**Bagus**	Three	**Tiga**
No	**Tidak**	Four	**Empat**
Room	**Kamar**	Five	**Lima**
Shop	**Toko**	Six	**Enam**
Sleep	**Tidur**	Seven	**Tujuh**
Toilet	**Kamar kecil**	Eight	**Delapan**
Yes	**Ya**	Nine	**Sembilan**
		Ten	**Sepuluh**

If you lose anything or have anything stolen, report it immediately to the police and get an officially stamped statement. Without this, most insurance companies will refuse to pay out claims money.

LANGUAGE

Bahasa Indonesia, which is the national language, is not only easy to pick up but will make your stay considerably easier and your experience of the country immeasurably richer. If you start with a few basic phrases before departure it won't take long to pick up new words and begin constructing simple sentences. Above is a list of useful words.

LAUNDRY/VALETING

Most hotels offer a fast and efficient laundry service with items returned the same day if they are given in before 9am. If you are in a real hurry, they can be laundered 'express service' and returned in as little as 4 hours.

LOST PROPERTY

If you lose something on a bus, train or in a public place, don't expect to get it back. Only in hotels and restaurants is lost property likely to be kept for a limited period of time.

MAPS

Several international cartographers produce good countrywide maps of Indonesia. For Jakarta, try to get hold of the Falk Map which is available at most local book shops.

MEDIA

Although Indonesia's media remain tightly controlled by the government, there are several English-language newspapers such as the *Indonesian Observer*, the *Jakarta Post* and the *Surabaya Post* which are available in the major towns. The *Asian Wall Street Journal*, the *International Herald Tribune*, *Time Magazine* and *Newsweek* are also widely available in leading hotels and major book shops.

These days, most big hotels offer satellite television with live broadcasts from Hong Kong and London, as well as nightly films and videos. Radio Republik Indonesia broadcasts programmes in English.

MONEY MATTERS

The Indonesian currency is denominated in rupees. Indonesian notes consist of Rp20,000 notes, Rp10,000, Rp5,000, Rp1,000, Rp500 and Rp100. Indonesian coins are Rp100, Rp50, Rp25, Rp10, Rp5 and Rp1 although these days the small denominations are rarely used. As a rule take smaller notes, as in many

Something for everyone

ARY'S TOURIST SERVICE CENTRE

We Provide :

- MONEY EXCHANGE AND SAFE DEPOSIT BOXES
- PACKING AND SHIPPING
- TICKETING RESERVATION: AIRLINE AND BUS
- SIGHTSEEING TOUR AND HOTEL RESERVATION
- RENTAL CAR AND TRANSPORTATION
- LICENSED POSTAL AGENT

JL. RAYA UBUD. UBUD 80571 BALI · INDONESIA · FAX (0361) 95162
TELEX NO. 35428 UBUD IA · PHN. (0361) 95162

places it can be difficult getting change for a Rp20,000 note.

The Indonesian rupee is freely convertible with other currencies, although in some of the more far-flung areas of Bali, Java and Lombok you may find foreign exchange banks hard to come by.

Bank Services

Local and foreign banks provide standard services nationwide. Banking hours are 8am–3pm, Monday to Friday, and 8am–1pm, Saturday. Money can also be changed at authorised money-changers and at hotels, although they may offer a lower exchange rate. Official exchange rates are published in the daily newspapers.

Jakarta has several international banks. Visitors who are heading to more remote areas of Indonesia are advised to change money and travellers' cheques in advance.

Cheques and Credit Cards

Thomas Cook MasterCard travellers' cheques free you from the hazards of carrying large amounts of cash, and in the event of loss or theft can quickly be refunded (see Emergency Telephone Number, page 180). US dollar travellers' cheques are recommended, though cheques denominated in any of the major currencies are also accepted. Major tourist and business hotels accept travellers' cheques in lieu of cash.

The following branch of Thomas Cook can provide emergency assistance in the case of loss or theft of Thomas Cook MasterCard travellers' cheques.
P T Thomas Cook Indonesia, *Jalan Wahid Hasyim 86, Jakarta.*

Foreign Banks in Jakarta

American Express, *Arthaloka Building,* *Jalan Jend Sudirman 2 (tel: 587 401).*
Chase Manhattan Bank, *Jalan Sudirman Kav 21 (tel: 578 2213).*
Citibank, *Jalan Sudirman Kav 21 (tel: 578 2007).*

NATIONAL HOLIDAYS

Indonesian national holidays vary from year to year, so you should always check with the tourist authorities or embassy. During public holidays, all forms of transport tend to get booked up.
1 January – New Year's Day
January/February – Mi'raj Nabbi Mohammed (Ascension of the prophet Mohammed)
March – Nyepi (Balinese New Year)
March/April – Lebaran (religious festival marking the end of the Muslim fast)
March/April – Good Friday
April 21 – Kartini Day (celebrates women's emancipation)
May – Waisak Day (marks the birth and death of the Buddha)
June – Idhul Adha (Muslim day of sacrifice)
June/July – Muharram (Muslim New Year)
17 August – Independence Day
August/September – Maulid Nabi Mohammed (Birthday of the Prophet Mohammed)
5 October – Armed Forces Day
25 December – Christmas Day

OPENING HOURS

Shopping centres, supermarkets and department stores are usually open between 9am and 8pm, Monday to Friday, and 9am–1pm on Saturdays, in the large cities. Government office hours are 8am to 3pm, Monday to Thursday, 8am to 11am on Friday and until 2pm on Saturday.

ORGANISED TOURS

Tour operators around the world offer a bewildering choice of package tours to Indonesia with the majority of them starting or ending at Bali with optional stays in Jakarta, Yogyakarta, Borobudur and Mount Bromo. These days, growing numbers of international operators like Trailfinders and Jetset Tours combine trips to Indonesia with other popular regional destinations such as Thailand, Singapore, Malaysia and Australia.

For those wanting greater freedom to move about at will, locally organised tours can also be arranged in almost every major town and city. Make sure that you use a reputable organisation though, as unauthorised guides abound. Best to ask at your hotel or in the local tourist office.

For details about available international tours, contact your nearest Thomas Cook office.

PHARMACIES

Pharmacies, known as *Apotiks*, can be found in almost all the main towns as well as many of the smaller ones. They generally sell a full range of all the items you would expect to find, from medicinal drugs and contraceptives to toothbrushes, shampoo and soaps. Although prescriptions are not generally needed for medicinal drugs, it is well worth knowing the generic name for any drug since they are often sold under different brand names. Also check the expiry date before purchasing a drug as they have a habit of staying on the shelves for a long time.

PHOTOGRAPHY

Indonesia is a veritable photographer's paradise. To ensure good results take your own film, since often what is available has been exposed to excessive heat. Keen photographers should take a polarising lens to reduce the glare and bags of silica gel to stop moisture getting into the camera. For really good results, concentrate on taking pictures in the early morning and late afternoon when the light is at its best. By midday, the heat and fierce shadows can spoil the most perfect shot. Generally you will be allowed free use of your camera. However, in some temples and museums you will be charged for taking in a camera or a video and in certain museums the use of flash is prohibited. If in doubt, ask at the entrance.

Local shops will process film in less than an hour, and at prices considerably cheaper than neighbouring countries. Don't expect high quality though. Despite the savings, it pays to get your pictures developed back home.

PLACES OF WORSHIP

Although some 87 per cent of Indonesians are Muslim, there are plenty of other religious groups too, including Roman Catholics, Methodists and Anglicans. The following places of worship can be found in Jakarta and Bali.

Jakarta
All Saints Church (Anglican), *Jalan Prapatan, Jakarta (tel: 345 508).*
Gereja Immanuel (Protestant), *Jalan Merdeka Timur 10, Jakarta Pusat.*
Jemaat Anugerah (Methodist), *Jalan Daan Mogot 100, Jakarta.*
St Canisius College Chapel (Catholic), *Jalan Menteng Raya 64, Jakarta (tel: 325 546).*

Bali
Maranatha Church (Anglican), *Jalan Surapati, Denpasar.*
St Joseph Church (Catholic), *Jalan Kepundung, Denpasar.*

Post office and box, Yogyakarta

POLICE

You will be able to recognise the regular Indonesian police by their khaki caps, their neatly ironed shirts and their proverbial smiles. For the most part they are extremely friendly, and almost to the man unable to speak English. To report loss or theft, either go to Jakarta's police headquarters on Jalan Sudirman 45 (tel: 587 771), or contact any other police office. Failing satisfactory progress, get in touch with your hotel or embassy.

POST OFFICES

Post offices can be found in almost all the main towns and villages, although they are generally extremely crowded and inefficient. A better option is to send mail through your hotel. When posting letters, make sure the stamps are properly stuck on, or better still, register them.

If you want to ship goods back home try to make arrangements through the shop where you purchased them. The

alternative is to take your package to the central post office, fill in various forms, have the contents verified, then wait several months in the hope that one day the package will turn up.

The General Post Office has its head office in Jakarta at Jalan Pos Utara 2, Pasar Baru (open: Monday to Friday, 6am–10pm; Saturday, 6am–1pm). On Bali, the head office is on Jalan Raya Puputan, Denpasar (open: Monday to Thursday, 8am–2pm; Friday, 8am–noon; Saturday, 8am–1pm).

PUBLIC TRANSPORT

By Air

Air transport is the easiest and most comfortable means of travel in Indonesia and there are flights to almost any provincial and district capital. For details, contact the following:

Jakarta

Bouraq Indonesia Airlines, *Jalan Angkasa 1–3 (tel: 6295 150)*.

Garuda Indonesia, *Jalan Sudirman 32 (tel: 570 6106)*.

Mandala Airlines, *Jalan Garuda 76 (tel: 420 6645)*.

Merpati Nusantara Airlines, *Jalan Angkasa 2 (tel: 417 404)*.

Sempati Air Transport, *Jalan Merdeka Timur 7 (tel: 348 760)*.

Bali

Bouraq Indonesia Airlines, *Jalan Sudirman 19 A, Denpasar (tel: (0361) 34947)*.

Garuda Indonesia, *Jalan Melati 61, Denpasar (tel: (0361) 34606)*.

Merpati Nusantara Airlines, *Jalan Melati 57, Denpasar (tel: (0361) 22864)*.

By *Becak*

Pronounced 'baychahk', this is an antiquated tricycle generally able to seat two people (although the locals occasionally squeeze in five), and is the perfect means of transport for short distances. Agree the price before you leave.

By *Bemo*

These illustrious minibuses pile in more passengers than you could dream possible and then proceed to stop frequently to pick up more. *Bemos* operate on almost all the main routes, and although generally cheaper than buses they take considerably longer.

Always check the destination and price, and if you are really in a hurry, rent the whole vehicle.

By Boat, see Island Hopping, pages 136–7.

By Bus

Buses are the most popular long-distance form of public transport serving most major towns and districts. Beware, however; while many of them travel like snails, others go like the wind and serious accidents are not uncommon.

For short trips there is little choice but to take the regular public buses which stop at every available opportunity, and will even do several circuits around town in order to pick up additional passengers. For longer trips, catch the express buses which rarely stop, are air-conditioned and on certain routes (Jakarta–Bogor) will use the toll roads.

Major towns often have several different bus stations, so always check prior to departure.

By Train

Train services may be considerably slower than the buses, but they do offer the advantages of greater safety and, in the first-class carriages, considerably more comfort. Trains leave Jakarta for Bandung, Yogyakarta, Surakarta (Solo) and Surabaya. Always try to buy tickets well in advance and make sure that at all times you keep your eyes on your luggage.

The Thomas Cook Overseas Timetable, which is published bi-monthly, gives details of many rail, bus and shipping services worldwide, and will help you plan a rail journey around Java. It is available in the UK from some stations, any branch of Thomas Cook, or by phoning 0733 268943.

STUDENT AND YOUTH TRAVEL
Student discounts are regularly offered in museums and in some guesthouses and hostels. Make sure you have an official card and photograph with you.

TELEPHONES
Local and international telephone services are available in most hotels and post offices. Note, however, that it is expensive to dial internationally and that hotels generally add a hefty surcharge.

International Codes for Direct Dialling:
Australia 61
Canada 1
Ireland 353
New Zealand 64
United Kingdom 44
United States 1

TIME
Java is 7 hours ahead of Greenwich Mean Time (GMT) while Bali and Lombok are 8 hours head of GMT. That means when it is noon on Java, it is 1pm on Bali and Lombok, 5am in London, midnight in New York and 3pm in Sydney.

TIPPING
In most tourist restaurants a 10 per cent service charge will automatically be added to your bill. Where it is not, tip in the region of Rp500–Rp1,000 if the service has been satisfactory.

TOILETS
Where there are tourists, there are normally sit-down loos. Otherwise, you will have to make do with the aptly named squat lavatory. If there is no

Local transport

flush, use the plastic dipper and bucket of water strategically placed alongside. To be on the safe side, take your own toilet paper, and if caught short, ask for the *kamar kecil*, or the WC (pronounced way say).

TOURIST OFFICES
Jakarta
Jalan Kramat Raya No 81 (tel: 310 3117-9).
West Java
Jalan Cipaganti 151, Bandung (tel: (022) 81490).
Central Java
Jalan Malioboro 14, Yogyakarta (tel: (0274) 62811).
East Java
Jalan Darmokali 35, Surabaya (tel: (031) 575 448-9).
Bali
Jalan Surapati Parman, Denpasar (tel: (0361) 22387).
Lombok
Jalan Langko No. 70, Ampenan (tel: (0364) 21866).

Indonesia Tourist Offices Overseas
US: 3457 Wilshire Boulevard, Los Angeles, California (tel: 213 387 2078).
UK: 3–4 Hanover Street, London W1R 9HH (tel: 0171 493 0030).

ACKNOWLEDGEMENTS
The Automobile Association wishes to thank the following photographers and libraries for their assistance in the preparation of this book: SPECTRUM COLOUR LIBRARY 6, 136, 156, 157.
The remaining photographs are held in the Automobile Association's own photo library (AA PHOTO LIBRARY) and were taken by Ben Davies for this book.

The author would like to thank: Guntur Purnomo, production manager of the Ramayana Ballet at Prambanan; the Borobudur Guesthouse; and the tourist authorities in Jakarta, Denpasar and Ampenan. Also thanks to Thomas Renaut in Bangkok.

CONTRIBUTORS
Series adviser: Melissa Shales **Designer**: Design 23 **Copy editor**: Rebecca Snelling
Verifier: Polly Phillimore **Indexer**: Marie Lorimer